Nursery Style

SERENA & LILY'S

Nursery Style

Serena Dugan & Lily Kanter

Foreword by Kate Spade

Photographs by Wendi Nordeck *Text by* Alison Singh Gee

CHRONICLE BOOKS

SAN FRANCISCO

Library of Congress Cataloging-in-Publication
Data available.

ISBN: 978-0-8118-5902-8

Manufactured in China.

Design by Satoko Furuta.

10 9 8 7 6 5 4 3 2 1

Chronicle Books LLC
680 Second Street
San Francisco, California 94107

www.chroniclebooks.com

To our husbands, Mike Dugan and Marc Sarosi,
whose unfailing support enables our labors of love.
To our mothers, whose faith and pride in us makes us believe
we can accomplish anything. *And to our fathers,* the
memories of whom inspire us to make an imprint on the world.

Contents

Foreword **9**
by Kate Spade

Introduction **10**

Chapter One
Defining Your Style **12**

Chapter Two
A Design Formula **28**

Chapter Three
Choosing Furnishings **50**

Chapter Four
Bedding & Textiles **80**

Chapter Five
Walls **100**

Chapter Six
Art & Accessories **114**

Conclusion **136**

RESOURCES **140**
ACKNOWLEDGMENTS **142**
INDEX **143**

Foreword

Not too long ago, even the most beautifully decorated homes all featured the same sort of standard-issue, boring nurseries. When my husband and I were planning for the arrival of our daughter, we kept thinking how we'd spent so much time making the rest of our home "us" and that we couldn't imagine designing a room that didn't fit. After some trial and error, we had a great time creating a warm, cheerful, and really fun room to welcome the newest member of our family.

Over the years other designers have caught on to this idea and now offer countless options, such as geometric patterned wallpapers, modern lacquered cribs, retro toys, elegant bedding, and amazing accessories. Even as a designer myself, all of the choices can feel a bit overwhelming to me. Happily, this wonderful book walks you through the process of design, color, and the intelligent placement of furnishings and accessories. Serena & Lily's take on style shows that a well-decorated nursery isn't always dictated by convention, but instead can speak to the diverse fashion sense and

ideas in all of us. *Nursery Style* can be used as a blueprint for a perfect baby room and guide to finding your inner designer.

Serena is a gifted artist and textile designer, and Lily once owned a wildly successful baby store in Northern California. When the two of them merged to form a bedding company, they brought back classics with a sophisticated twist. So often in stores you'll find luxurious fabrics without the variety of design, or interesting, colorful design without the quality, but Serena and Lily were thoughtful on both accounts. Their bedding collections for the nursery are filled with hand-embroidered birds and flowers, large melon damasks, chocolate dots, madras plaids, cabbage roses, and classic houndstooth—all of which I adore and are as soft as can be.

Nursery Style does a great job of giving us permission to break the rules. It's an absolutely beautiful book—I only wish had been written just a few years earlier!

Kate Spade

Introduction

The birth of a baby means a rebirth for the family: A child enters the world; a woman becomes a mother; a man becomes a father; partners become parents. And guess what? That guest room or home office is reborn as a nursery, the space in which you nurture a new life. A nursery is not just the baby's room—a place for sleep, changing, and storage—but also the space in which you will spend so many of your waking moments for the next few years—an essential family room. For that reason, the nursery needs to be a little universe where you love to be. Beautiful. Tranquil. Practical. Pleasing to the baby and true to the design integrity you've established throughout your house. After all, your baby is a part of you. Shouldn't his or her room be an extension of your style, reflecting all the beauty and comfort you would expect for yourself?

Creating a nursery is an exciting challenge. It can manifest as your vision of the perfect childhood. A place where the past (your beloved Eames rocking chair) meets the present (where do I stash these diapers?) meets the future (could a vintage globe inspire a future world traveler?).

As you begin creating your baby's nursery, we encourage you with this idea: Most babies don't have an opinion about their surroundings until they are two—and then they'll weigh in often and loudly—so enjoy the luxury of creating a room that fits your vision. Our hope is that this book will help you think outside the nursery box. While you await your little one, explore all the options for feathering your nest.

As designers, trust us: There's no need to fill the room with floor-to-ceiling cartoon characters or a matching suite of all-too-tasteful baby furniture, if that's not what you want. You can craft this space with original art, flea-market finds, and that crib you fell in love with from the boutique down the street.

In these pages, we offer you stylish solutions to practical nursery issues and inspiration for creating a space that reflects who you are as a family.

"Have fun. Be fearless. Stay true to what you love!"

chapter one

defining your style

DESIGN DIRECTION | THE CLASSIC NURSERY | THE VINTAGE NURSERY
THE MODERN NURSERY | THE ECLECTIC NURSERY | GET THE LOOK

NO DOUBT, YOU'RE EMBARKING ON ONE OF THE GREATEST JOURNEYS OF YOUR LIFE: RAISING A CHILD. And since you've picked up this book, we're going to assume that you want to do this with a certain élan. Don't feel intimidated by those four bare walls, the curtainless windows, or that pile of baby gifts accumulating on the floor of what you've designated as the nursery. We're here to help you create the family haven you've always imagined.

Do start your planning early. Allow yourself months, rather than weeks, to create this room, so that it can evolve over time into something unique, a place that reflects your sensibilities, rather than a space that was rushed into being. Starting early will afford you the luxury of wandering flea markets and faraway boutiques to find key pieces that truly speak to you.

What's more, if you decide to custom-order bedding, artwork, or furniture, starting months before the baby's arrival will ensure that items arrive in time. Trust us: Nothing's worse than stressing over an unassembled crib or that specially made, but as of yet undelivered, bumper while your third-trimester hormones are swirling. Give yourself the grace of time.

"We're here to help you create the family haven you've always imagined."

design direction

"Your particular design direction will act as the foundation of your nursery."

That said, take your time with the all-important first step: defining your style. Your particular design direction will act as the foundation of your nursery. Even if you haven't consciously decided what that might be, your preferred style is probably already visible in your home.

Take a good look at your favorite room. Is your living room, for example, filled with beautiful antiques and traditional prints such as florals, checks, and stripes? You may well gravitate toward a classic look. Do you prefer furniture with clean lines, few frills, and graphic textiles? Most likely, you gravitate to a modern aesthetic. Did you choose a couch with a shabby-chic vibe and a secondhand coffee table with a wonderfully timeworn feel to it? There's a good chance you love the vintage look. Or maybe you prefer to fuse styles and eras, mixing your great-aunt's antiques with furniture and artwork from your travels throughout the world. If so, you're probably a fan of the eclectic approach to design.

While there are myriad design influences, we've found that there are four major styles of nursery: Classic, Vintage, Modern, and Eclectic. These general classifications can serve as a guide for developing your own individual design style. With this in mind, you can either choose one look and follow it through or blend interesting pieces from different genres to create your own statement. We firmly believe that there is only one true rule in creating a nursery: This is a place that should be unique to your family.

left: **A WHITE LEATHER, MOROCCAN-STYLE POUF** LENDS ITSELF TO THE EXOTIC OR ECLECTIC NURSERY.

above: **THIS DISTRESSED FINIAL** HINTS AT THE HISTORICAL.

left: **A PAINTED FRENCH CANE-BACK BERGÈRE** IS UPHOLSTERED IN A CASUAL CREAM COTTON CANVAS FOR CASUAL WEAR.

right: **A GLAMOROUS LUCITE VANITY STOOL** FROM THE SEVENTIES MAKES A COMEBACK.

THERE IS ONLY ONE TRUE RULE
IN CREATING A NURSERY:

*This is a place that should be
unique to your family.*

the classic nursery

The Classic Nursery is a traditional American baby's room, with furniture in shapes that we're all familiar with. Here, you might find a lovely sleigh crib, an upholstered glider and ottoman, and a rocking horse for decoration. The color palette is generally soothing, with soft pastels such as light blue, pink, green, lilac, and yellow. Walls might feature nursery rhyme artwork, family photos, or children's paintings. Baby's first shoes or decorative blocks would make perfect

"Many parents choose a classic nursery because that is what their own nurseries were like."

accessories in this room. The silhouettes, textures, and patterns in the Classic Nursery are comforting in their familiarity; they do not challenge or jar our sensibilities with progressive design aesthetics. Many parents choose a Classic Nursery because that is what their own nurseries were like. The time-honored brings an invaluable sense of comfort with it: Parenthood is a monumental challenge, and the Classic Nursery is a reassuring place.

top left: **BIRD PANELS OVER THE CHANGING TABLE,** FABRIC ANIMAL CUTOUTS OVER A DOOR, AND GENTLE KNIT TOYS SIGNAL THIS IS A KID-FRIENDLY SPACE.

bottom left: **SOFT AND COLORFUL KNIT TOYS** LIKE THIS SWEET STRIPED BUNNY LOOK ADORABLE PROPPED ON A BED PILLOW OR BLANKET.

the vintage nursery

"Flea-market finds such as old wooden clocks
or handmade toys complete the vintage look."

This baby room more assertively looks toward the past, creating an aura that is heirloom. Each piece in the Vintage Nursery should look as though it were made by hand. Jenny Lind–style cribs, with their intricate-looking spindles, were most likely the cribs our parents slept in as babies. They are still sold today, designed to suit the most current safety standards, and they come in a variety of colors and finishes. Other vintage-style cribs feature lovely touches such as an appliqué of carved-wood flower garlands or swags, which lend them an old-world feel. Often, the edges and slats of vintage-style cribs are softened with a rubbed-paint finish or distressed to expose some of the wood. Pieces such as the armoire and changing table can be actual sturdy antiques, or they can be new but with an added patina to look old. The vintage color palette is typically soft and "washed": a tea-stained ivory rather than bright white; silvery sage rather than lime green; rose rather than fuchsia. The typical vintage color palette reinforces the timeworn feel in the Vintage Nursery. Consider accessorizing with gilded, beveled, or etched mirrors to lend a romantic air. Warm the floors with woven or latch-hook rugs that look homemade, accessorize the glider with a crocheted throw or quilted blanket, and hang a chandelier in the center of the room. Flea-market finds such as old wooden clocks or handmade toys complete the vintage look. This is a nostalgic nursery, one that tugs at the heartstrings and transports the family to a simpler time.

design tip:

Go on a scavenger hunt for vintage and reproduction wallpapers, fabrics, and other products online. A growing number of creative textile artists are fabricating the charming prints of yesteryear.

NO. 1

A SWEET BIRD-AND-FLORAL RELIEF ON A CRIB PANEL AND A WELL-LOVED, CREAM, APPLIQUÉD SPREAD SLUNG OVER A WHITE CRIB RAILING KEEP VINTAGE DECOR LOOKING FRESH.

the modern nursery

The modern era of design evolved in the 1950s and was based mostly on the principle that form should follow function. Thus, the Modern Nursery doesn't feature frills, ruffles, or extraneous decoration. Furniture lines are simple, clean, and minimal. A modern crib looks sleek and well designed. Textiles and art are often bold and graphic—think a framed Pucci scarf or a Rothko print on the wall. Lighting can take on striking organic shapes: A textured Noguchi paper lantern in the place of a chandelier would provide a cool finishing touch. The color palette in this room is typically more audacious: a healthy dose of white paired with stronger, vibrant colors. The best Modern Nursery will temper design purism with practicality: We love the look of a sleek, retro rocking chair for the Modern Nursery. But, for the sake of comfort during those midnight feedings, we'd probably smother it in sheepskin throws.

"Furniture lines are simple,
clean, and minimal."

left and top right: **A DARK WALNUT AND WHITE LACQUER CRIB** ANCHORS AN OCEAN-WASHED ROOM. THE NEW BREED OF MODERN CRIBS ARE AKIN TO HIGHLY SOUGHT-AFTER BAUHAUS PIECES; THEY STAND ON THEIR OWN.

bottom right: **WHIMSICAL TOYS** COLORING THIS MODERN NURSERY SOFTEN THE EDGES OF A CLEAN DECOR.

EXOTIC IS UNITED WITH CLASSIC AND VINTAGE IN A NURSERY STARRING FAUX-PAINTED CHINOISERIE WALLS. GLOBAL ACCENTS, SUCH AS THE JAPANESE WOODEN DOLLS, BATIK-PRINT COMFORTER, AND FOLKSY APPLIQUÉ PILLOWS CAN ALL PEACEFULLY COEXIST.

the eclectic nursery

"The Eclectic Nursery has a fearless, unique, border-hopping sensibility."

This is the baby room in which several design aesthetics—modern, classic, vintage, and ethnic—beautifully coexist, a personal take on the nursery that is totally fresh and original. The Eclectic Nursery has a fearless, unique, border-hopping sensibility, with bohemian touches such as a cashmere blanket from India and intriguing mementos from around the globe. This space is about bringing together unexpected elements from different time periods and diverse parts of the world and setting them amid a surprising color palette. Nothing here matches in the expected way—the dresser, armoire, and crib are not all built from the same predictable honey-colored wood. Yet, everything harmonizes beautifully. We love the daring juxtaposition of a salmon-colored crib, a white Chinese wedding chest, and celadon walls. Add a chinoiserie-inspired mural, layered Oriental rugs, and paper lanterns to drive home a dazzling and original design message.

get the look: AUDACIOUS VINTAGE

This nursery is truly vintage, but with a twist: The layering of the different floral designs found in the wallpaper, art, and bedding gives the room an "over the top" appeal that feels fresh and daring, not stodgy.

focal point » WALLPAPER

This original 1920s stripe-and-floral wallpaper is a design statement in itself and pointed the way for the rest of the room's furnishings.

Art: Vintage floral oil paintings on floral backgrounds give a pop of color, breaking up the wallpaper background, reinforcing the vintage look, and continuing the layering of those flowers.

Crib: An old-school, Jenny Lind–style crib is traditionally vintage. Pink keeps things sweet.

Bedding: These modern, simplified floral shapes assert a slightly daring design sensibility by breaking the rigid "vintage" style of the room while remaining consistent with the established color and theme.

Rug: A sweet hand-hooked rug ties together the color palette, softens the expanse of the hardwood floor, and adds a touch of the handmade, which gives "vintage" its character.

chapter two

a design formula

DESIGN | BEDDING | WALLS | AN HEIRLOOM | ARCHITECTURE
COLOR PALETTE | COLOR COMBINATIONS | GET THE LOOK

NOW THAT YOU'VE IDENTIFIED YOUR DESIGN DIRECTION, YOU'RE READY TO MOVE FROM INITIAL INSPIRATIONS TO REALITY. The first step is research: What's available in stores, on the Internet, in your home? Seeing great nurseries in books, magazines, friends' homes, and on television will enlarge your vision, as well.

Browsing baby boutiques on the Internet is an easy and stress-free way to source the ever-expanding market of beautiful furnishings and bedding. Knowing what's out there will help you choose products that speak to you on a personal level. And let's face it: This approach saves you the hassle of getting your blossoming body dressed and coaxing your swollen ankles into your suddenly too-tight shoes.

As you research your options, you might also want to consider the furnishings and artwork already in your home. Perhaps a painting from the living room or a chest from the master bedroom would look beautiful and function well in the nursery.

At this stage, you will also want to think about what mood you envision for your baby's room. Do you want it to be sweet? Funky? Whimsical? Is there a nursery from a favorite movie or book whose spirit you would love to capture? Keep in mind that mood differs from design style in that it creates the ambience, not just the style, you desire. For example, parents who have decided on a Modern Nursery

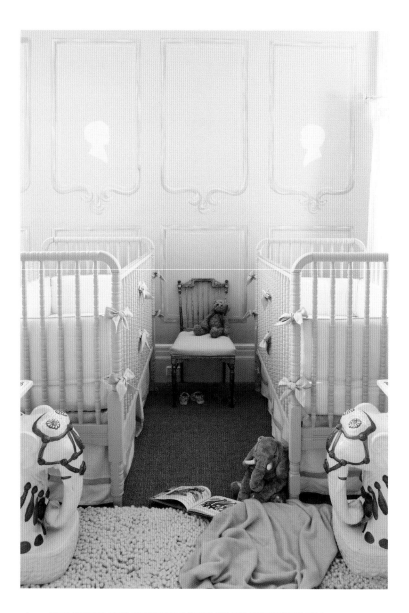

"Knowing what's out there will help you choose products that speak to you on a personal level."

for their baby girl could opt for a sweet mood and incorporate lilac walls, white lacquer furniture, and a flokati rug. Or they could choose a cool, funky vibe and use white walls as a clean canvas for a bold color combination such as fuchsia, burnt orange, and moss green, which could be introduced with textiles, bedding, and accessories. A colorful abstract painting that picks up this palette would underline the ambience the parents are after. Ceramic elephants in a Classic Nursery would give it a whimsical mood, whereas an heirloom doll collection might make it feel more nostalgic. Clarifying the feel of the nursery from the start should make your furnishing and art choices that much easier.

Perhaps the most important question to answer before you embark on designing your room is this: Will you know your baby's sex before the little one arrives? If so, do you want to create a distinctly feminine or masculine space? If you're leaving that glorious surprise for the day of your child's birth, you might want to consider a neutral room to which you can add special gender-based touches after your baby joins you.

right: **A PORCELAIN INDIAN ELEPHANT GARDEN STOOL** IS STATIONED AT THE FOOT OF THE CRIB, ATOP A VERSATILE WHITE PILE RUG LAYERED OVER WOOL SISAL CARPET.

A DELICATE SHELL CHANDELIER SUSPENDED FROM A PITCHED CEILING SHIMMERS IN THIS AIRY SPACE AND INSPIRES THE WHITE-ON-WHITE COLOR PALETTE. STACKED WHITE LEATHER POUFS—TOOLED WITH MOROCCAN MEDALLIONS—ARE EASY TO PUSH AROUND.

design AS THE FOCAL POINT

Once you've established your design direction, looked for inspiration, considered the furnishings available to you, and pondered the mood you want to create, you are ready to choose your design focal point.

We have friends who have created focal points from things as disparate as 1920s Eiffel Tower statuettes, floral-patterned wallpaper by William Morris, an old hand-carved wooden Chinese screen, and a hand-painted

"What is a design focal point? It is the standout item that is the star of your nursery."

What is a design focal point? It is the standout item that is the star of your nursery; whether a piece of furniture, a work of art, or an heirloom, it is that special item, architectural element, or color combination that attracts the eye the moment a visitor walks into the room. It is a design detail that both anchors the nursery and sparks ideas for selecting the color palette, textiles, and remaining furniture. Simply put, a design focal point is that extraordinary design element that inspires the rest of the nursery.

floral Bombay dresser. If the color combination you choose for your room is striking, it too can serve as the room's focal point, sparking other design decisions.

Combined with your design direction, a design focal point will lead you to choose your color palette, artwork, and furnishings. So, as you wander flea markets and boutiques, or even study old photographs of your family home, stay in tune with which statement-making bedding, paintings, or special pieces of furniture truly inspire you.

bedding AS THE FOCAL POINT

*"The bedding, serving as the focal point,
 prompted our color direction . . ."*

When designing for our clients, we often start with bedding as a focal point, as it is commonly the first thing parents-to-be fall in love with, and it is a natural inspiration for the room's color palette.

For one client's decidedly boyish Eclectic Nursery, we chose jaunty crib bedding done up in a bold plaid of orange, aqua, and navy. The bedding, serving as the focal point, prompted our color direction—orange, varying shades of blue, and white—which manifested in several aspects of the room. To complement the preppy spirit of the bedding, we chose a classic white crib. But a matching changing table proved too safe a choice. Instead, we shook things up by taking a stainless steel industrial kitchen prep-table and placing a changing pad on

it. A seamstress helped us create a white-and-orange canvas runner with roomy pockets to drape over the table, adding warmth while keeping changing supplies and toys within arm's reach. This innovative addition gives the room a fresh and unexpected appeal. The crib and changer are vastly different in design style, but, unified by a distinct color palette, the pairing feels harmonious.

To splash more color into the room, we painted the ceiling sky blue and laid a graphic orange-and-white–striped rug on the floor. A whimsical blue-and-white painting of the family's beloved dog personalizes and sweetens the space. The overall effect of the nursery is clean, bold, and sporty.

top left and right: **A PALE BLUE CEILING AND ORANGE-STRIPED RUG** CONVEY A FEELING OF SAND AND SKY.

bottom left: **CRISP, CLEAN CUSTOM PANELS** WITH GROMMETS CONCEAL A STORAGE AREA AND COORDINATE WITH THE JAUNTY MADRAS BEDDING. THE ORANGE IN THE PANELS IS REPEATED AS CONTRAST WELTING ON THE AQUA BUMPER AND TACKED ON AS TRIM FOR THE CRIB SKIRT.

walls AS THE FOCAL POINT

A splashy wallpaper pattern of oversized white paisleys on an elegant gray background inspired a girl's Modern Nursery, steering the furniture choices toward a crib with spare lines and a changing table with complementary white-and-dark– stained wood. The allover pattern makes a strong statement and creates a sense of environment, with the focal point enveloping the room because it is on all four walls. Simple but sumptuous

> *"Mod paisley wallpaper directed the style of this nursery."*

lilac-and-white bedding injects a dose of color into the room. A Lucite side table with curvy legs feels both modern and feminine, and an ornate Venetian glass mirror completes the look by echoing the intricate detailing of the paisley wallpaper and creating an interesting fusion of design styles. Whether this effect is created through wallpaper, decorative pattern painting, or mural, walls as a focal point give a room instant wow and make it feel one-of-a-kind.

TEA FOR TWO IS A CHIC AFFAIR WITH THIS VINTAGE LUCITE SIDE TABLE AND WHITE FLOKATI RUG.

design tip:

Need help creating perfect
polka dots for a decorative wall
treatment? Use the lid from a
gallon of paint as your template
and trace it onto your wall.
The scale is perfect.

NO.2

an heirloom AS THE FOCAL POINT

Let's say the baby will be a girl, and dad wants his mother's polka-dot rocking horse to inspire the nursery. Here's how such a well-loved heirloom would work as a focal point. The horse's polka dots suggest a graphic theme, an echoed pattern throughout the vintage–eclectic room. Mom chose a hand-painted polka-dot pattern for the walls and sweet polka-dot bedding for the crib. A vintage-feel rug punctuated by red accents unifies the color statement. A romantic white crib adds to the nostalgic mood of the nursery, as does furniture with patina—an antique daybed, vintage side tables, and a timeworn vanity converted into a changing table. A bold leather-framed mirror with a round looking glass supports the polka-dot pattern in a fresh way; this unexpected element shoots a dash of the modern into the room, keeping the mix lively.

Take note as to how this decorating approach places the wonderful passed-down rocking horse at the center of attention but decidedly avoids any one theme. The design message here is personal and thoughtful, and it emphasizes what is meaningful to this family.

FRENCH-STYLE FURNITURE MERGES WITH AN HEIRLOOM ROCKING HORSE, MODERN UPHOLSTERED OCTAGON MIRROR, CLASSIC CRIB, AND NEEDLEPOINT RUG IN THIS SWEET ROOM—A QUINTESSENTIAL ECLECTIC NURSERY.

architecture AS THE FOCAL POINT

Your nursery might have some standout architectural features that you'd like to showcase. For example, an angled ceiling and beautiful Gothic window in one baby's room created the perfect alcove for a crib. The parents wisely wanted to make the most of such lovely built-in details. Thus, they chose a muted color palette that quietly complemented the room and opted for simple,

"Celebrate the room's unique built-in features . . ."

elegant furnishings. A white sleigh crib with bedding that accented the walls and a classic white glider were selected so that no design statement overpowered that of the architectural details. This Classic Nursery feels graceful and balanced, celebrates the room's unique built-in features, and serves as a great example of how architecture can provide a natural focal point. Paneling on the wall or ceiling, or bold crown molding, can also become the star of a room, accented by wallpaper or painted insets.

left: **EXISTING ARCHITECTURAL ELEMENTS,** SUCH AS THE GOTHIC WINDOW AND PITCHED CEILING, BECOME MORE PRONOUNCED WHEN ROOM COLORS ARE MUTED.

above: **A LOVELY DECORATIVE CHAIR** WITH SMALLER PROPORTIONS CAN BE A USEFUL NURSERY PIECE. SECONDARY SEATING THAT'S MOVABLE AROUND THE ROOM WILL FIND A NUMBER OF PURPOSES.

color palette AS THE FOCAL POINT

Sometimes parents will find themselves devoted to a color palette: Maybe you simply can't resist the allure of a pink nursery for your little girl or a blue room for your baby boy. We say, go with what you love. A chosen color makes a natural focal point. The next logical step is to select bedding you love and then find furniture that showcases your design direction.

One mother-to-be fell in love with the blue-and-white color scheme of a block-print tablecloth she picked up during a memorable trip to India—so much so that she transformed the border of the tablecloth into a bed skirt for her baby's crib and another piece into a matching Roman window shade. That choice led to a lovely blue-and-white palette for the entire

"Consider what mood you're going for before you commit to a hue."

nursery: soft white walls with a blue border, classic white furnishings, a delightful homemade painting of a blue bouquet, and a blue-and-white porcelain elephant stool, which punctuates the room's subtle ties to India. The rest of the tablecloth was put to good use and turned into basket liners and drawer pulls, weaving together the color-palette focal point. Remember that the color scheme you choose invariably affects the mood of the nursery. Blue, for example, has a calming effect. Yellow is cheery. Red adds excitement. Pink often reads as sweet. Some colors, such as pinks, reds, and oranges, warm the space; others, such as blues and greens, make

A BLUE-AND-WHITE BLOCK-PRINT TABLECLOTH FROM INDIA WAS USED TO MAKE THIS ONE-OF-A-KIND CRIB SKIRT. AN ARTIST WAS COMMISSIONED TO PAINT THE FLORAL IMAGE OVER THE SLEIGH CRIB, WHICH REINFORCES THE COLOR PALETTE.

the space cool. Consider what mood you're going for before you commit to a hue. Then head to the paint store to pick up tester sizes of different shades of your chosen color and try them on the nursery walls. Live with the various shades for a few days, noting how they look in natural light and by lamplight, before you make your decision.

COLOR PALETTE STEERS ALL FURNISHING CHOICES IN THIS NURSERY.

color combinations

To use color skillfully, consider the way that different colors combine with one another to create visual impact. You probably remember the color wheel from your grade school days. The color wheel shows each color's relationship to another, starting with the primaries of red, blue, and yellow, then the secondary colors, such as orange, green, and purple, and so on. A basic understanding of color theory is sufficient to hone your design skills and help you use color to achieve a feeling in a room.

A HANDFUL OF QUICK LESSONS:

- Colors that are opposite one another on the color wheel, such as blue and orange, are called complementary colors and look great together.

- Colors that are similar to one another, called analogous colors, also look nice together if they have a similar level of color purity or intensity. For example, violet and periwinkle blue—the range of colors in hydrangea flowers—look gorgeous together because their undertones harmonize with one another.

- Add lighter or darker shades of a color to your palette to make it richer. For example, if you are using shell pink and sprout green (two complementary colors), bring in a darker value of the same pink, such as watermelon pink, to make the combination more interesting.

Some unusual combinations we love:

boy color combos	effect	design direction	see example
	• GRAPHIC • FRESH • FUN	MODERN OR ECLECTIC	PG. 22
	• CRISP • BOYISH • BOLD	VINTAGE OR CLASSIC	PG. 49
	• SPORTY • LIVELY • GREGARIOUS	ECLECTIC OR MODERN	PG. 35 & 113

girl color combos	effect	design direction	see example
	• SOFT • DEMURE • SWEET	CLASSIC OR VINTAGE	PG. 40
	• PUNCHY • AUDACIOUS • CHEERFUL	ECLECTIC OR MODERN	PG. 84
	• SOPHISTICATED • STYLISH • CALMING	MODERN OR CLASSIC	PG. 37

neutral color combos	effect	design direction	see example
	• SOOTHING • INVITING • QUIET	VINTAGE OR ECLECTIC	PG. 79
	• QUIRKY • COOL • HIP	MODERN OR ECLECTIC	PG. 108
	• PUNCHY • CLEAR • FRESH	CLASSIC OR MODERN	PG. 19

Sometimes finding a design focal point is effortless: You've already fallen in love with that knockout crib or armoire, or maybe you've had your heart set on hanging that beloved oil painting in the nursery. But sometimes you might have to search a little longer to find something that truly inspires you. The moment you find it, you will more than likely experience an "Aha!" moment, a rush of excitement, a singing of the Muses.

Keep in mind that the focal point is only one aspect of developing your larger design formula, but once you settle on your focal point, choose your color palette, and articulate your design direction, you will be well on your way to selecting the furniture, textiles, and other unique touches for this special room.

HAND BLOCK-PRINTED INDIAN FABRICS IN FLORAL PATTERNS OFFER ENDLESS VARIATIONS ON A CHOSEN COLOR PALETTE.

design strategy

○ DETERMINE YOUR DESIGN STYLE:
Modern, Vintage, Classic, or Eclectic.

○ DECIDE THE MOOD OF THE ROOM:
Sweet, Bold, Quiet, or Nostalgic.

○ KEEP GENDER (or gender-neutrality)
IN MIND.

○ CHOOSE YOUR DESIGN FOCAL POINT.
IDENTIFY YOUR COLOR PALETTE.

○ CHOOSE FURNITURE, TEXTILES,
AND WALL TREATMENTS.

○ CHOOSE ARTWORK AND DECORATIVE
ACCESSORIES.

get the look: VINTAGE COOL

The Union Jack is an international symbol of hipness, and its graphic blue, red, and white design is a great source of inspiration. Timeworn accessories create a sense of history and, like that favorite pair of blue jeans, give the room a cool vibe.

focal point » RUG

This Union Jack rug delivers a confident, graphic punch and offers up a distinct color palette. The rug's red stripes are echoed in the crib, curtain ties, and decorative accessories. Splashing red throughout the room balances the visual impact of the rug.

Custom curtains: Bands of red make these made-to-order burlap curtains pop.

Crib: A crib painted an unusual color injects a shot of the unexpected into this nursery.

Artwork: Vintage letters from commercial signs emphasize the retro vibe.

chapter three
choosing furnishings

SLEEP | CHANGE | FEED | STORE | GET THE LOOK

YOU MIGHT BE SURPRISED, AND RELIEVED, TO DISCOVER THAT NURSERIES REQUIRE LITTLE FURNITURE. A well-functioning, streamlined room with just the right pieces makes the strongest design statement and keeps clutter at bay. What's more, expanses of floor space, warmed by beautiful rugs, will come in handy once your little one starts to crawl. All this is good news for parents-to-be—fewer pieces to fret over, more time to devote to finding furnishings you adore.

When it comes to thinking about nursery furniture, you need only consider four main actions: SLEEP, CHANGE, FEED, and STORE.

[FEED]   [SLEEP]

[CHANGE]

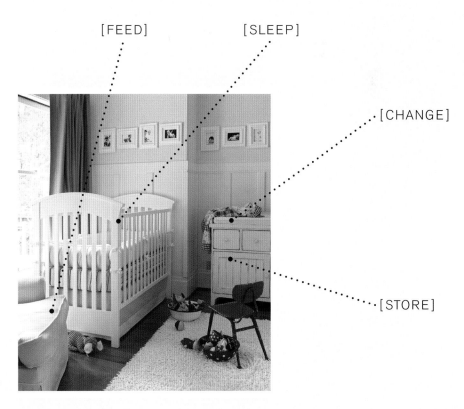

[STORE]

sleep

"Think about your child's sleep needs for both now and over the next few years."

For so many parents, a crib will be the most important purchase for the nursery, and understandably so. The crib will be the baby's physical and emotional home for the first few years of his or her life, and it's the most iconic item in the nursery.

Cribs are now offered in a seemingly endless array of silhouettes and finishes. Your choice will depend not only on the design style and palette you've selected for your nursery but also on the level of functionality you desire. Think about your child's sleep needs for both now and over the next few years.

The first thing to consider regarding a crib is drop gate versus fixed rail. Standard American cribs include a drop-gate railing, which you can lower with one hand while you carry the baby with your other hand. Fixed rails are the standard in Europe and are becoming increasingly popular in America as modern-style cribs from the Continent become more popular; fixed rails mean less visible hardware, which works well with the modern aesthetic. These cribs are typically lower to the ground than the American standard.

Many infant-furniture companies are introducing oval and round cribs. These shapes offer an alternative to the standard rectangular crib and fit well in smaller spaces. They do, however, require specialized bedding.

Consider, too, the lifespan of a crib. For example, most cribs are useful solely for the first two to three years of a child's life. But a convertible crib transforms into a toddler bed by removing the crib's front panel and putting a guardrail in its place. The conversion kit will most likely cost extra but will extend the life and usefulness of the crib. The downside of this choice is that a convertible crib might in fact look like a crib that's doing double duty as a bed.

If functionality is your top concern, then you've narrowed your search considerably. If style is your priority, then prepare to be spoiled by choice. Give yourself plenty of time to explore the online baby boutiques and the catalogs that are no doubt flooding your mailbox to find the perfect crib for you. Applying your design style to the equation may help with your selection. However, don't worry if you've realized that you are classic in style and you've fallen head over heels for a modern crib. Dare to shake things up. Finding pieces that you love and blending disparate looks and textures is what our nursery style is all about.

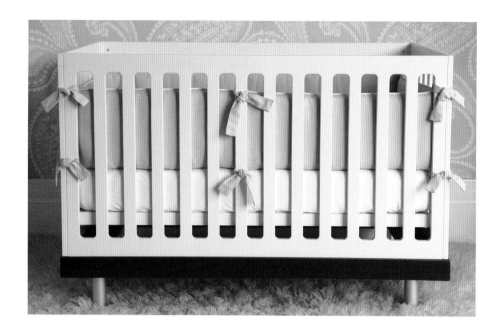

above: **A FIXED RAIL ON A CRIB,** SUCH AS THE ONE ON THIS MODERN WOOD-AND-LACQUER MODEL, STAYS PUT.

right: **A DROP-GATE CRIB** MAKES IT EASY TO GET BABY IN AND OUT.

Crib Safety:

While vintage cribs may look lovely, they can be a safety hazard. Years of previous use can wear down a crib's joints and a safety rail's locking mechanism, and cribs sold prior to 1986 do not adhere to current U.S. safety regulations. Better to opt for a new crib in your preferred style—there are myriad new cribs that have been designed to look antique.

classic crib

Style:

SLEIGH

CLEAN & LINEAR

What makes it that style?

· Traditional lines, familiar to adult home furnishings

· Subtle decorative elements with minimal embellishment

vintage crib

Style:

JENNY LIND

IRON

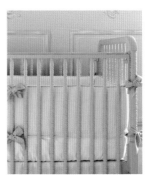

What makes it that style?

· Turned spindles (carved posts), which are reminiscent of past eras

· Appliqués (raised carvings) of decorative details, like floral garlands and swags

· Distressed, aged, or rubbed paint finishes, displaying a timeworn patinated finish

· Iron rails and finials

modern crib

Style:

FIXED-RAIL

GEOMETRIC

What makes it that style?

· Simple, linear design

· Typically lower to the ground, with no drop gate

· Little, if any, detailing, aside from geometric design elements

eclectic crib

Style:

TRADITIONAL

TRADITIONAL

What makes it that style?

Any crib style works with the Eclectic Nursery. What makes it eclectic is the context. An out-of-the-ordinary paint finish or unexpected bedding choices create the surprise element that makes the room eclectic.

change

The moment you bring your little one home, you will realize the importance of having a comfortable and functional spot to change your baby's diaper. Trust us on this one. As a parental duty, diaper changing comes second in importance only to feeding. So, we say, why not opt for a changer that is both functional and easy on the eyes?

In terms of utility, your changing center should not only have a place for a changing pad, it should also offer a home for fresh diapers and related essential items. For this reason, standard changing tables are a natural option, but certainly not the only one.

Your changing station should be roughly 34 to 42 in. (86 to 107 cm.) high and should accommodate a standard contoured changing pad at 16 in. wide and 34 in. long (40 cm. wide and 86 cm. long). Other pad sizes and shapes are available, but this is the standard to which most covers are made. Choose a changing station that has open shelving—bonus points for drawers to store onesies, booties, and blankets, as you'll need to keep such everyday clothing within arm's reach. If you decide to purchase a standard changing table from a baby store, consider its adaptability. Ideally, the appeal and function of the piece would endure past your child's infant years; once the changing pad and any safety lip are removed from the top, the changer should be able to serve as a dresser in your child's room or elsewhere in the house.

An alternative choice would be a stylish dresser that you can convert to a changing table by adding a changing pad and Velcro or a trimmed rug-pad (this will keep the changing pad from slipping, though you should never leave your child unattended on a changing table). Perhaps you already own such a dresser and simply need to repurpose it for the nursery. A paint job, new knobs, and graphic drawer linings can give an old piece of furniture new life.

An armoire also has the potential to become the perfect changing station. Look for one that has a shelf deep and wide enough to hold a changing pad and that can be pulled outward for this purpose. Many well-crafted children's furniture lines offer armoires with such a feature; alternatively, a skilled carpenter could add a sturdy reinforced retractable shelf to an armoire you already own. A piece such as this would allow you to stash extra essentials out of sight.

"Don't limit your purchase to a store-bought changing table. Look for a dresser, desk, or table with a surface large enough to accommodate a changing pad."

A DISTRESSED, FREESTANDING CHANGING TABLE WITH PLENTY OF DRAWERS
COULD EVOLVE FROM CHANGING TABLE TO STORAGE SOLUTION WHEN BABY GROWS
OUT OF DIAPERS.

THIS WORKSTATION, BUILT INTO A CLOSET, CONVERTED TO A PERFECT CHANGING STATION.

CHANGING TABLE
checklist

You've probably gotten heaps of baby-gear advice from everyone from your mother-in-law to the salesperson at your local baby boutique. We have our own list of tried-and-true basics to keep within arm's reach of the changing table. Use this as a guideline for how to stock and organize necessities before the baby arrives.

○ **CLOTH DIAPERS:** If you decide to use washable diapers, make room for four dozen cloth diapers and eight diaper covers.

○ **DISPOSABLE DIAPERS:** Stash a large boxful in the closet, but keep two dozen within arm's reach, arranging them in a basket or bin next to the changing pad or on a nearby shelf.

○ **WIPES:** Whenever you need diapers, you will certainly need wipes or washcloths. Trust us on this. Have on hand two dozen soft washcloths or one box of disposable wipes (we recommend the unscented/no-alcohol version). A wipes warmer ensures that cloths are at a comfortable temperature when they reach your baby's bottom; if you choose to use one, make sure you place your changing table near an electrical outlet.

○ **DIAPER PAIL OR RECEPTACLE:** Just south of the changing table, you'll need a receptacle for dirty diapers, whether that is a diaper pail (basically, a special airtight trash can with a lid) or a special appliance that wraps up used diapers and stores them until you empty it. Plan to empty either type of container daily to keep the nursery fresh.

○ **NEWBORN ESSENTIALS:** Diaper barrier cream, aspirator, infant thermometer, and nail clippers.

○ **LIGHTING:** A dimmer switch for your main light source makes midnight diaper changes more comfortable for baby. If you do not install a dimmer, place task lighting—a small lamp with a 40-watt bulb works well—next to the changing table. Make sure that the light illuminates the area but does not shine into your child's eyes. Also, keep the lamp cord out of reach.

If your chosen changing table doesn't have shelves or drawers, consider installing shelving nearby, although not directly above the changer (for safety reasons). A row of hooks can hold frequently worn clothing or such comforting items as soft blankets.

left: **AN INDUSTRIAL RESTAURANT PREP-TABLE** SERVES AS A CHANGING TABLE WITH A MODERN TWIST.

right: **ADD BASKETS TO A DESK OR DRESSER** AND PLACE A CHANGING PAD OVER A NONSKID LINER TO PRODUCE A UNIQUE PIECE OF CHANGING FURNITURE.

far right: **EXISTING BUILT-IN BOOK-SHELVES** NOW SERVE AS A CHANGING NOOK. WICKER BASKETS HOUSE DECORATIVE PILLOWS AND TOYS. HANGING OBJECTS MOBILE-STYLE OVER THE PAD HELPS DISTRACT BABY AS YOU TAKE CARE OF BUSINESS.

Changing Table Safety:

Keep in mind that when the baby is able to sit or stand, any objects
above a diaper changer should be nonbreakable.
(Most ideas on this page are suitable for babies up to 6 months.)

feed

"You should keep in mind that your glider offers yet another opportunity to add a distinct design touch to your nursery."

The rocking chair of nurseries past has certainly evolved. The standard was once a wooden spindle rocker; then the padded glider took its place. Today, the state-of-the-art nursing chair is a fully upholstered and slipcovered chair that glides and swivels. All three versions are still available on the market, but we recommend the third option for comfort as well as looks.

Approach this purchase like you would all others in your baby's room: functionality first, but with design as a priority, too. You should keep in mind that your glider offers yet another opportunity to add a distinct design touch to your nursery. Most gliders are upholstered to a customer's specifications. You can request such details as contrasting piping, which we love, incorporate fabrics from your bedding or curtains, or introduce a colored fabric that matches a piece of artwork in the room. For practicality's sake, we recommend looking for a chair with a removable, washable slipcover cut from preshrunk fabric. It should look well tailored without seeming too fussy or high maintenance.

Matching ottomans are not only stylish, but immensely useful. Many doctors recommend that mothers put their feet up while they nurse. A lumbar pillow adds back support and, cut from the right fabric, can splash more of your color palette into the room. If anyone else will be assisting with feeding the baby, make sure the glider accommodates the height of that person. If you have the space, a daybed is a gracious touch, both lovely to look at and a soothing option for a nursing mother to share with her baby.

When it comes to choosing chairs for your visitors—be it a sibling, a grandma, or even a favorite teddy bear—you should feel free to have a little fun. Secondary seating could come in the form of a chair, bench, daybed, or even child-sized chairs, and it's a seamless opportunity to add some design dash. For example, in a girl's Modern Nursery, a small Lucite table and a padded bench add the perfect design touch and a welcoming spot for visitors. In a Vintage Nursery, one trip to the flea market will yield countless options. Look for interesting shapes and sturdy construction. Reupholstering and a new paint job can revitalize and customize even the shabbiest piece, as long as the chair's bones are strong. The only rule to follow here is to choose a piece that makes your heart sing. Dare to break the rules with this addition to the nursery.

left: **NATURAL-FIBER, UPHOLSTERY-WEIGHT FABRICS** ARE BEST FOR SLIPCOVERED GLIDERS.

above: **THIS STYLISH NURSERY** INCLUDES AN UPHOLSTERED FRENCH-STYLE DAYBED THAT LETS YOU NURSE LYING DOWN.

"When it comes to choosing chairs for your visitors—be it a sibling, a grandma, or even a favorite teddy bear—you should feel free to have a little fun."

Furniture Safety:

An inexpensive lead test can determine whether your flea-market find—be it a chair, lamp, or accessory—contains lead-based paint. If it does, either remove it from the nursery or have a professional strip and refinish it.

SPARE CHAIRS ALLOW FOR EXTRA SEATING. WINDOW SEATS, OTTOMANS, POUFS, AND BENCHES ALL DO THE TRICK.

store

Babies are magnets for stuff, and in the first few months, grown-ups are almost fully to blame for that. After all, who can resist showering an adorable little one with all sorts of toys, keepsakes, and clothes? For that reason, organized storage is essential for the nursery.

Storage options, chosen thoughtfully, can accentuate your design direction. For example, baskets can be lined with fabrics that coordinate with your bedding or window treatments. Toy boxes come in vintage, classic, and modern shapes. You might also want to call into service an antique trunk, chest, or suitcase. Painted ice buckets can catch heaps of toys and look charming at the same time.

An armoire is a striking element that not only makes a statement but also provides a stylish home for treasured baby dresses or jackets. A bookshelf is another useful addition to the nursery. Not only can it house the bedtime books that your baby will so enjoy, it can also showcase such poignant items as silver monogrammed cups, framed baby photographs, and heirloom treasures. Keep books on a lower shelf so that your growing child will one day be able to grab favorite reads by him- or herself, and arrange framed pictures and other breakables above. Open shelving can also accommodate color-coordinated boxes of varying sizes, which can serve as a perfect storage solution for small toys and odds and ends.

Thoughtful friends and relatives will no doubt shower your baby with clothing, some of it for when your newborn grows a little bigger. If you have the room, you would be wise to purchase two dressers—one to accommodate newborn clothes, the other for larger-sized outfits for the future. If your nursery can accommodate only one chest of drawers, keep the too-big garments in airtight plastic boxes marked with sizes: 3 to 6 months, 6 to 9 months, 9 months to 1 year, etc. These boxes can be stashed in the closet and can later house outgrown clothing to be given away or saved for a future sibling.

"Organized storage is essential for the nursery."

left: ONE TOY STORAGE OPTION IS **OLD FLOUR SACKS.** THEY'RE GREAT FOR TODDLERS WITH TOYS GALORE.

ADD A BOHEMIAN TOUCH TO A DRESSER BY KNOTTING COORDINATING FABRICS INTO PULLS.

above: **BOTTOM DRAWERS ARE IRRESISTIBLE TO TINY HANDS,** SO STORE SOFT LINENS AND CLOTHING WHERE BABY MAY REACH.

right: **ELEGANT STORAGE.** THIS FRENCH-STYLE NIGHTSTAND NEAR THE CRIB HAS A DRAWER AND CABINET FOR A FAVORITE BOOK OR WARM THROW.

BUILT-IN STORAGE IS A WORTHWHILE INVESTMENT: IT SAVES FLOOR SPACE AND CAN
ADAPT AS BABY GROWS.

ARMOIRES ARE AMONG THE MOST VERSATILE OF HOME FURNISHINGS. WELCOME ONE
INTO THE NURSERY AS STORAGE FOR CLOTHES, BLANKETS, SHOES, BOOKS, AND TOYS.

design tip:

Head to a gardening store and purchase rubber lawn and leaf bins as colorful, unexpected storage for toys.

NO. 4

A LUCITE MAGAZINE RACK IS REVIVED AS A BOOK
AND TOY BIN FOR A CHIC, MODERN NURSERY.

get the look: CLASSIC CHIC

Hand-painted silhouettes of a twin boy and girl make the nursery feel one-of-a-kind and elegant. The decorative painting, both whimsical and chic, creates symmetry and marks out space for each baby. The soft but not overly feminine color palette provides a perfect backdrop for a gender-neutral babies' room.

focal point ›› DECORATIVE PAINTING

The Parisian-inspired faux molding adds personality, while also breaking up the visual expanse of this large wall. The hand-painted silhouettes reinforce the concept of "his" and "hers" and give this Classic Nursery a certain sweetness.

Crib: These cribs were painted the same color as the wall, in a satin finish. This helps the cribs "disappear" into the background of the wall.

Tip: JENNY LIND–STYLE CRIBS ARE OFFERED IN AN UNPAINTED FINISH, MAKING THEM EASIER TO CUSTOMIZE.

Elephant side tables: Unusual exotic items, such as these ceramic elephants, fascinate babies and become the iconic images of childhood. These elephants make a spectacular design statement and reinforce the symmetry in this twin nursery.

chapter four

bedding & textiles

CHOOSING YOUR BEDDING | WINDOW TREATMENTS
FLOORING | GET THE LOOK

THE TEXTILES IN YOUR NURSERY—CRIB BEDDING, WINDOW TREATMENTS, GLIDER UPHOLSTERY, AND RUGS—ARE AN ESSENTIAL STATEMENT IN THE OVERALL DESIGN OF THE ROOM. Textiles provide a sense of warmth and texture. They boost your design direction and add a graphic splash. If a single bold fabric captivates you, you can allow it to take center stage as your focal point. Or your textiles can play a supporting role in the design of your nursery, complementing your color palette or focal point.

While color will surely be your starting point, remember to explore the tactile aspects of fabrics in the nursery. Crisp cottons will keep your baby comfortable in the crib, while you might want to indulge in a soft cashmere throw for your glider. Nubby rugs feel soothing under bare feet. A silky faux-suede glider can be a cozy perch for a midnight feeding. And best of all, a fuzzy teddy bear makes a tender friend for a baby.

A STUNNING STRIPED PEONY QUILT ON THE FLOOR MAKES A COZY SPOT FOR NEWBORN PLAYTIME.

A DELICATELY APPLIQUÉD COTTON FELTED BLANKET MAKES FOR A MODERN YET ORGANIC ACCENT TO BABY'S ROOM.

HAND BLOCK-PRINTED TABLECLOTHS FROM INDIA INSPIRED THE DESIGN DIRECTION OF THIS NURSERY.

TRY TICKING STRIPES FOR A BOY'S NURSERY: THEY'RE CLEAN AND CLASSIC AND MIX WELL WITH OTHER FUN PRINTS OR BASIC SOLIDS.

choosing your bedding

At Serena & Lily, the nursery begins with bedding, allowing the rest of the room to fall seamlessly into place. The pattern and color combinations of well-designed bedding provide a natural focal point and inspiration for the rest of the nursery. You may have a paint scheme and color palette in mind before you choose your bedding. That's no longer a problem with so many delightful bedding choices on the market. It shouldn't be hard to find a crib set that matches your color theme. Crib sets now come in audacious color combinations, such as chocolate brown and shell pink, or dynamic pattern juxtapositions, such as giant florals and stripes. Such large statements easily spark other design ideas. Crib bedding typically consists of a bumper, a fitted crib sheet, and a crib skirt. Many parents also add a waterproof pad that protects the mattress and the crib linens. The bumper is placed inside the crib to protect the baby from injuring herself on the crib slats. Bumpers come in a variety of shapes and sizes, but for the sake of practicality, you might want to consider a slipcovered one for easy washability.

A crib skirt can add a finishing touch. A tailored skirt looks crisp and sleek, while a ruffled skirt has a more playful appeal. Most cribs have multiple height settings that you adjust as the baby grows (the lowest setting is to prevent a bigger baby from climbing out of the crib). To keep the skirt from pooling onto the floor

HAND-EMBROIDERED FLORAL DETAILING ENLIVENS A STRIPED CRIB SHEET.

as you make these adjustments, call upon crib-skirt pins, available at baby boutiques and on the boutiques' Web sites. You can also have the skirt shortened at your local dry cleaner for relatively little cost.

A baby quilt is another warm and welcome addition to a nursery; it can be hung on the wall as decoration when your child is a newborn and then used as a blanket when he or she becomes a toddler. Monogrammed blankets personalize a

"At Serena & Lily, the nursery begins with bedding."

room and make treasured keepsakes. You can also choose embroidery styles to match your chosen design direction, an added visual statement when draped over the glider.

If you do have your heart set on particular bedding, choose accessories and other furnishings to showcase the fabric, allowing its pattern and color combinations to pop. For example, if your crib bedding has a distinct pattern, keep the rug, curtains, and glider fabric simple and color-coordinated. We opt for color-contrasting accents, such as banding on curtains, and lampshades and piping on upholstery. Strong contrasting hues, perhaps in the rugs or throws, can set off the supporting colors in the bedding.

Bedding Safety:

Loose materials such as blankets, pillows, and stuffed animals present a suffocation hazard for babies. They should only be used as decoration when the baby is elsewhere and should never be left in the crib while the baby is lying down. The crib's fitted sheet should have a tight, secure fit and should wrap underneath the mattress so the baby cannot pull it off. Crib bumpers should be securely tied on the outer slats so that a baby cannot loosen them, and bumper ties should be no longer than 14 inches long to avoid possible strangulation. If you do decide to hang a quilt on the wall next to the crib, make sure it is securely fastened to the wall.

above: THINK OUTSIDE THE BOX. **A SEARCH FOR UNUSUAL FABRICS** LED TO AN ONLINE AUCTION SITE AND A GORGEOUS BLUE-AND-GREEN IKAT PRINT THAT WAS EASILY CONVERTED TO A BABY QUILT—ONE YOU'D NEVER FIND AT A BABY STORE!

right: **A CUT COTTON CHENILLE BUMPER** ADDS VISUAL INTEREST TO A PEACHES-AND-CREAM PASTEL NURSERY.

window treatments

"Curtains present yet another fun opportunity to tell the design story of your nursery . . ."

Curtains present yet another fun opportunity to tell the design story of your nursery, especially if you customize yours to incorporate the fabrics from your bedding and glider.

Roman shades are a great custom option that can be constructed from almost any fabric or material, such as bamboo, linen, or cotton. When used in the baby's room, we recommend an outside mount for greater light control. Curtain panels can be cut from fabrics you have already chosen for the room. Another stylish look is panels cut from white canvas and accented by a two-inch banding in either a contrasting color or a coordinating pattern.

With almost every style of curtain, we prefer to add either blackout lining or additional roller shades (inside the window frame) of blackout material so that you can adjust the amount of light filtering into the room. Bamboo Roman shades underneath curtains look fresh and add texture, and they also block out sunlight.

Of course, prefabricated curtains are also a fine choice, although you will not have the option of incorporating your bedding or glider fabric, unless offered by the manufacturer. Floor-length curtains can also be hemmed, if necessary, so they are just skimming the floor. We recommend avoiding curtains hemmed just below the window if your window does not go to the floor, as curtains in the middle of the wall visually chop up a room.

Shutters are a practical and charming choice: They have a fresh, clean look and can be adjusted to block out light and control the room's ventilation and temperature. A traditional choice for historical houses, shutters are well suited to a Classic or Vintage Nursery.

right: **DECORATIVE CURTAINS** CAN BE SHEER TO ALLOW FOR DIFFUSED LIGHT, BUT ROLLER SHADES SHOULD BE ADDED INSIDE THE WINDOW FRAME FOR NAPTIME.

far right (top): **BLACKOUT LINER** CAN BE ADDED TO CURTAINS FOR MAXIMUM LIGHT CONTROL.

far right (bottom): **CANVAS PANELS WITH GROMMETS** KEEP THE NURSERY SHIPSHAPE—AND ARE EASY TO MOUNT.

	curtain style	customize by	guidelines
roman shade		SEWING ON A 1½ IN. RIBBON OR BIAS-TAPE BORDER.	FOR A CLEAN LOOK: • SEW AS CLOSE TO THE CURTAINS' EDGE AS POSSIBLE. • MITER THE CORNERS (MEETING THE RIBBON DIAGONALLY AT THE CORNERS, LIKE A PICTURE FRAME).
		ADDING COLORFUL BALL-FRINGE OR TASSEL-TRIM ALONG THE BOTTOM.	• THIS LOOKS BEST WHEN PAIRED WITH A VERY CLEAN, TAILORED SHADE. • WRAP THE TRIM AROUND THE BACK OF THE SHADE WITH A HAND-STITCH.
curtain panels		CUTTING SOME LENGTH FROM THE BOTTOM OF THE PANELS AND REPLACING IT WITH AN ANCHORING BAND OF CONTRASTING FABRIC.	• ALLOW TWO FEET OF CONTRASTING FABRIC TO SHOW, HITTING RIGHT AT THE FLOOR. • SEW NEW FABRIC TO ORIGINAL PANEL WITH MATCHING SEAMS.
		SEWING ON A 1½ IN. RIBBON OR BIAS TAPE FRAME.	• A GRAPHIC FRAME CAN BE CREATED WITH A SINGLE OR DOUBLE ROW OF RIBBON OR BIAS TAPE. • MAKE SURE YOU LEAVE THE SAME AMOUNT OF SPACE AROUND ALL FOUR SIDES OF THE FRAME.

right: THERE ARE AS MANY WAYS TO CUSTOMIZE STORE-BOUGHT WINDOW COVERINGS AS THERE ARE NURSERIES. THIS **COTTON ROMAN SHADE** WAS "TATTOOED" BY A HENNA ARTIST.

far right: **SHADES MADE FROM RENEWABLE NATURAL RESOURCES,** SUCH AS THE BAMBOO SHOWN HERE, MAKE GREAT SENSE FOR THE NURSERY AND THE ENVIRONMENT.

Curtain Safety:

Be sure that the crib is not directly next to a window. Not only does this keep baby away from drafts, but it also keeps your little one away from curtain cords, which present a strangulation hazard. When choosing window treatments, opt for those with circular cords, not loose, hanging ones. Any excess cord should be wound up with a tie. Also make sure that brackets are securely fastened to the wall and rods are sturdy so that a toddler grasping onto a curtain panel cannot pull the hardware down. If adding any accessories to the curtains, make sure they are securely fastened so as not to pose a choking hazard to a curious toddler.

Short
and tall

flooring

If your nursery has wall-to-wall carpeting and you are planning to keep it in place, remember to consider it when choosing your color palette. If your carpeting is a neutral color, you're in luck. You can simply layer rugs on top of it in hues and patterns that punctuate your color palette. However, you should plan to professionally clean the carpet before baby arrives, to remove all allergens and stains.

Designwise, hardwood, cork, and natural linoleum floors make a more striking showcase for your chosen rugs, and, ultimately, it is more convenient and less costly to roll up a rug and take it to the cleaners than to hire cleaners to work on a carpet. So if you have the choice, you might want to opt for rugs on top of attractive flooring.

> *"If your carpeting is a neutral color, you're in luck. You can simply layer rugs on top if it."*

Rugs are not only an easy way to warm up a room, they make a great visual anchor and also act as a sound buffer for hardwood floors. Through color, texture, and pattern, a rug will literally and figuratively "ground" the space. If you call upon strong patterns for the bedding, curtains, or upholstery, you might want to stick to a rug with a simple and complementary charm. If your nursery textiles don't feature any major patterns, then

left: **A GREEK KEY-PATTERN WOOL RUG** EMERGES AS CLASSIC ART IN AN OTHERWISE QUIET SPACE.

above: **A BOTANICAL-PRINT RUG** PAIRS BEAUTIFULLY WITH TRADITIONAL COTTON DAMASK UPHOLSTERY.

left: **EXOTIC RUGS** USUALLY FOUND IN THE LIVING ROOM OR STUDY CAN BE BORROWED FOR THE NURSERY WHEN FORGING AN ECLECTIC DECOR.

right: **FLOKATI** IS A GORGEOUS TOUCH IN MOST WELL-APPOINTED ROOMS, INCLUDING THIS HIP NURSERY WHERE IT CAN CUSHION LITTLE FALLS. IT MAKES AN ULTRASOFT STATEMENT WHEN SERVED UP WITH DELICIOUS HUES OF PEACHES AND CREAMS.

far right: **WOVEN AND HOOKED RUGS** COME IN FUN SHAPES AND SIZES—GOOD FOR PLACEMENT NEAR A CRIB.

certainly try out a graphic rug in the room. A unique rug may well be your focal point. In your chosen color palette, such a rug can offer the space a welcome and unifying jolt.

Remember, different rug styles reinforce different design messages. Flokati, sheepskin, and shag rugs feel funky and modern. Keep in mind that while flokati and sheepskin rugs may seem impractical because of their white color, they can be taken to a professional cleaner. If such measures seem too demanding, a shag rug in a deeper color requires less maintenance but still adds heaps of style.

Oriental rugs take the room in classic and heirloom directions. Animal-print rugs add an exotic and eclectic air. Sisal rugs are understated and can be woven into any design scheme. It's fun to trim them with a

fabric border or layer them by throwing another rug on top. And don't forget to consider the softness factor of your chosen rug since this is undoubtedly where your little one will crawl, sit up, fall, and explore. Be sure to take off your shoes in the store to try out your selection.

A note on nursery hygiene: Some parents establish a slippers-only rule in the nursery, not only to keep floors clean but to avoid tracking outdoor pollutants onto rugs, where baby will do much exploring. Expect to clean your rugs at least once yearly, and choose a professional who uses environmentally friendly, nontoxic detergents. You can also air your rugs outside in between cleanings.

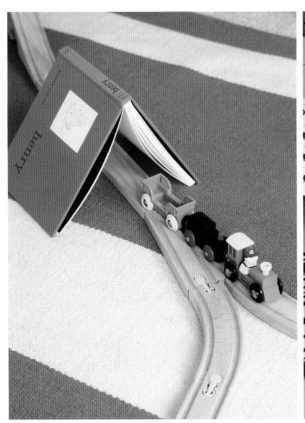

far left: **SPORTY ORANGE STRIPES** FINISH THE ROOM WITH FLAIR.

left: **FAUX-ZEBRA THROWS,** SUCH AS THIS WOOL DHURRIE, TAKE ON A MOD FEEL WHEN LAYERED OVER WALL-TO-WALL WOOL SISAL.

right: WE ADORE THIS **VIBRANT, WOOL VERSION OF THE UNION JACK,** WHICH LOOKS MASCULINE ON THE DARK-WOOD FLOOR.

Rug Safety:

Natural-fiber rugs, such as those made of cotton, silk, and wool, are most highly recommended for nurseries. Carpets made of polyester and acrylic can give off harmful fumes. If you choose an antique rug, be sure to have it professionally cleaned to remove all allergens and loose threads. Be sure to air the rug afterward to remove any chemical smells. For children with allergies, doctors recommend keeping the nursery free of any kind of rug.

get the look: INTERNATIONAL VINTAGE

A block-printed Indian tablecloth inspired this nursery's design and China-blue-and-white color palette, a color combination embraced by countries throughout the world. The crib skirt was cut from the decorative border of the inspirational tablecloth; the remaining cloth was turned into a Roman shade. These two textiles anchor the color palette.

focal point >> COLOR PALETTE

Bright white on the walls, furnishings, and floor provides a perfect canvas for bold blue highlights throughout the room.

Art: The light hand of this painting gives it a weathered appeal, which makes it the perfect complement to the washed and airy room. The blue, white, and natural hues strengthen the room's color palette.

Accessories: The carefully chosen accessories in this nursery all tie in to the focal point: color, with a worn, casual, international feel. Wooden clogs, hand-made toys, and a carved painted vintage chair all have a lived-in yet worldly feel. Design details like the knotted fabric drawer pulls are an unexpected touch.

Bedding: The strong blues and intricate pattern on the crib skirt make the skirt this crib's visual anchor, grounding it in an all-white room. An airy white sheet and bumper disappear into the white walls, while the periwinkle ties create a quiet pop of color.

chapter five

walls

THE POSSIBILITIES OF PATTERN | SOLID-COLORED WALLS | THE RIGHT COLOR
THE RIGHT TONE | THE RIGHT SHADE | GET THE LOOK

WALLS CREATE THE AMBIENCE IN YOUR NURSERY, WHETHER YOU SEEK AIRINESS, WARMTH, WHIMSY, OR DRAMA. Solid-colored walls in a striking and well-considered hue make just as big a statement as decorated walls. Indeed, the appropriate wall treatment communicates your design vision and will make the single biggest impact on the mood of your room. What's more, walls act as the backdrop to your furnishings, allowing your room's focal point to take center stage.

Keep in mind that walls done in different textures and finishes convey different messages: Wallpaper adds depth and visual interest. Beadboard wainscoting feels vintage. Molding creates a sense of history and architectural interest. Paneling breaks up the room and adds character. Decorative painting provides limitless possibilities for expression.

Before you choose a wall treatment, however, you might find it immensely helpful to choose your bedding or the most boldly patterned textiles first. Parents often have strong reactions to textiles: Often bedding, splashy rugs, or patterned curtains are the first elements of the nursery

"Once you've settled on your textiles, your wall treatment should fall easily into place."

that capture your heart. It is infinitely easier to match a wall treatment to a textile than to coordinate a textile to an unusual wall pattern or color palette. Once you've settled on your textiles, your wall treatment should fall easily into place. Then, with your wall treatment as a canvas, it's easier to choose the rest of your furnishings. Of course, there are exceptions to this rule—maybe the existing molding or wallpaper in your nursery will inspire your other choices for the room. But when in doubt, follow the above-mentioned order. That said, let's consider the particular joys of both patterned walls and solid-colored walls and also the process of choosing a paint color that's just right for your nursery.

PATTERNED WALLPAPER GUIDES THE TAUPE-AND-WHITE COLOR PALETTE IN THIS NURSERY, MAKING THE TASK OF ACCESSORIZING EASY.

design tip:

Try painting the ceiling an accent
color and leaving the walls white.
Rooms with paneling, especially,
don't need colored walls.

NO.5

the possibilities of pattern

"The primary ways to create pattern on your walls are decorative painting and wallpaper."

Pattern on the walls creates an instant presence and gives your room intimacy and character. Pattern can enliven the space, and contrary to what you might have heard, deep colors and graphic patterns are right at home in a small nursery. It can make your room feel warm and nurturing and can give a space presence, regardless of size.

The larger the scale of the pattern, the more likely it will become your room's focal point, with the rest of your furnishings taking on a supporting role. The same is true of a colorful pattern. A tighter pattern with a tonal palette (varying shades of one color), which might feel more textural than heavily patterned, can easily blend in with the room, offering more subtle interest. This allows another design element to become the star of the show. A great rule to consider—the smaller the pattern or the closer the shades of color, the subtler the pattern

will seem. Another rule to keep in mind: When mixing multiple patterns in a room, vary their scale. Keep the color palette connected while finding different distinct yet harmonious scales and motifs, such as pinstripes and florals or stripes and checks in varied scales.

The primary ways to create pattern on your walls are decorative painting and wallpaper. One of the great advantages of decorative painting is the flexibility it affords. You can choose any design, scale, and color combination and truly tailor the pattern to create a unique room. What's more, hiring a professional to paint patterned walls can be less costly than wallpaper and professional installation. Just be sure to ask the artist to provide you with a sketch or small mock-up on paper, to test on the wall before committing to the job. We love the handcraftsmanship and artistry visible in

CHAIR-RAIL MOLDING DIVIDES THE WALL AND LETS YOU PAIR FUN PATTERNS, SUCH AS **THE ENGLISH-ROSE PRINT AND PINK-AND-WHITE PINSTRIPES SEEN HERE.** CROWN MOLDING ADDS ARCHITECTURAL FINISHING.

design tip:

Vertical stripes are a fun
way to break up a large
expanse of wall.

NO. 6

decorative painting. Indeed, it's a design feature in its own right. The imperfect, handcrafted, one-of-a-kind qualities of such a job, whether done by you, your child, a friend, or a hired artisan, have immeasurable beauty. This work can be done freehand or with the help of guides like stencils and tapes. Plus, when your child is ready for a change, it's easy to paint over your work.

Wallpaper, on the other hand, offers the distinct benefit of "what you see is what you get." Pinning up strips of your chosen wallpaper will give you a good idea of how the pattern will look in your room; clearly this is not something you can do as easily with decorative painting. If you envision an intricate design or a tight allover pattern, your better choice is wallpaper; the more elaborate the design you desire, the more cost-prohibitive the hand-painted job will be. Don't be swayed by the old notion that wallpaper is too sweet or staid. Not only does it have a great deal of retro charm (ideal for a Vintage or Classic Nursery), but depending on the pattern, it can breathe cool new air into an otherwise predictable modern space. Also keep in mind that wallpaper does not have to be vinyl to be practical. Just look for a paper that bills itself as washable.

BRANCHES FROM THE FLORAL BEDDING SERVED AS INSPIRATION FOR THE ASIAN BRANCH, BLOSSOM, AND PAGODA VISUAL ON THE NURSERY WALLS.

DOT ON DOT: POLKA DOTS LAYER WELL AGAINST ONE ANOTHER AS LONG AS THE COLORS HARMONIZE AND THE SCALE VARIES.

HOW TO USE PATTERNS ON THE WALLS:

rules of thumb

○ The more similar the colors in a pattern are to one another, the more subtle—and less likely to make a bold statement—the walls will be.

○ The more disparate the colors in a pattern are, the more attention-grabbing the pattern will be, probably making the walls your focal point.

○ The smaller the scale of the pattern, the more it will recede into the background, making it seem more like texture and less like a declaration of style.

○ The larger the scale of the pattern, the more likely the walls will become the focal point, with the pattern taking on a forceful presence.

○ Wall pattern can successfully echo other patterns in the room if the scale is varied. For example, stripes can work beautifully with other stripes in a room if they complement rather than match each other, thus giving a sense of layering. Choose patterns in harmonious colors to build on the beauty of the patterns rather than detract from them.

○ Wall pattern can also coordinate with other patterns in the room by providing a pleasing contrast. Rather than seeming busy, the right coordinate can ground a pattern. Example: Think of adding a trellis, woven, or bamboo pattern to a floral pattern. Remember to match colors and overall design style to make this pairing effective. The general rule here is to make sure that your coordinate complements rather than competes with the primary pattern.

solid-colored walls

A painted wall in an appealing, solid shade can make the perfect backdrop for your furnishings and artwork, particularly if you want to spare your focal point any visual competition. Beautiful color is a design element in itself: Basic white can tell a story. Just the right shade of petal pink can instantly sing softness and sweetness. You will want to explore the shade (lightness versus darkness) and the tone (the mixture of colors within one color). For example, there are tonal differences between tomato red, which has a shot of yellow in it, and rose red, which contains more blue. These subtle aspects of color can make or break your room, so we'll show you how to choose just the right hue. Paint color, well chosen, shouldn't attract attention on its own; it should create the mood, rather than act as focal point, of your room.

"A painted wall in an appealing, solid shade can make the perfect backdrop for your furnishings and artwork…"

RICH TURQUOISE WALLS MAKE TOUCHES OF CHOCOLATE BROWN AND ORANGE POP IN THIS GROOVY NURSERY.

the right color

To narrow down your wall-color choices, start with the color palette that comes from your focal point. This will serve as your guide. For example, say your focal point is a pale pink, watermelon, sprout green, and white quilt. Which color from this palette is right for your wall? Don't assume that the wall color has to be the most neutral or subtle color in the palette. Begin by asking yourself what mood you want to strike. Do you want your room to feel girlie and sweet or vivacious and out of the ordinary? A girlie ambience might be created by choosing pale pink or white; watermelon and sprout green would communicate vitality and something out of the ordinary. Also ask yourself which color you prefer. Choose the one that you'll continue to love from winter to summer and as your baby grows into a toddler.

Color truly transforms a room: It affects your mood and your comfort level. A properly chosen wall color will put you at ease and buoy your spirits. A color selected because you thought it coordinated well, or because it was what you thought you were supposed to like, will haunt you. You will never feel fully at home in this special room if you don't adore your paint color, so go for the one that makes your heart skip a beat.

top right: **EMPHASIZING THE SOFTER TONES IN YOUR COLOR PALETTE** CREATES A GENTLE, SWEET NURSERY.

bottom: **FOCUSING ON THE RICHER COLORS IN YOUR PALETTE,** WHILE CONTRASTING THOSE COLORS WITH WHITES OR OFF-WHITES, CREATES A BOLDER STATEMENT FOR THE NURSERY.

the right tone

"You'll be surprised at how different a color looks when splashed onto four walls."

You've chosen the color you love, but that's just the beginning, as we've all learned the hard way. It's all too easy to get the exact tone wrong, wrong, wrong: Yellow that looks like a highlighter. Pink that gives you a cavity. Green reminiscent of that old taffeta bridesmaid's dress. This is not what you'd had in mind for your nursery! A "toned" color is one that has been softened with a grounding hue, typically brown, to make it appear less brilliant. While this may not sound pretty, a toned, mellowed version of a pastel color makes that color more inviting. So-called "cleaner colors," while beautiful on fabric, can be harsh to the eye when covering four walls. A toned color looks more sophisticated and makes an otherwise jarring color feel lush and remarkably livable.

If you aspire to match your walls to a color in your bedding or a favorite textile, use that color as a starting or reference point, rather than trying to match it exactly. You'll be surprised at how different a color looks when splashed onto four walls; sometimes a beautiful color simply looks too intense when it's surrounding you. Best to sample a few shades from the same color family and see which feels right to you.

color specialists:

Home magazines often reference paints in their resource sections. If you spot a potential paint color while flipping the pages, jot down the brand and specific name or number. Take it to the paint store; if it's not the exact hue you're looking for when you see it in person, an employee at the store can recommend one that might suit you better. Most specialty paint store professionals are extremely skilled with color; their over-the-counter advice is free, educational, and reassuring. What's more, if you're still not confident, these specialists can refer you to a colorist (a decorator who focuses on selecting hues). The colorist comes to your house with a color wheel, checking the effects of natural and artificial light in the room, and suggests appropriate colors. This consultation takes a couple of hours and costs relatively little money compared to wasted paint and effort.

the right shade

"We strongly recommend swatching at least three paint colors of varying shades and tones."

Selecting the right shade of color is, mercifully, the easy part. Some general guidelines to keep in mind: Lighter colors create a softer, sweeter feeling. Medium to darker shades have more presence and create more of a statement; they also allow for greater contrast when paired with whites or off-whites.

As with choosing the right tone, choosing the right shade requires sampling. We strongly recommend swatching at least three paint colors of varying shades and tones. If you're overwhelmed by choosing a color, rest assured that testing colors helps make the right choice clear. Even seemingly identical paint chips will manifest as vastly different colors on the wall, when seen in context and painted as a large swatch. If your nursery has molding, try painting a two-coat swatch in a three-foot-by-three-foot square against it; this way you can see how the woodwork contrasts with your chosen color. To get a further read on the color, obstruct your view of the adjacent unpainted walls by holding up two pieces of paper at the edge of the swatch—this blocks out the view of any existing wall color, which will interfere with your interpretation of the new color. If you think you've settled on a favorite, sample a larger patch. Then apply a smaller patch of this same color to another wall to see how it looks in a different light. Take a few days to reflect on your selection at different times of day. Once you're happy, you've found your color. WHEW!

what to look for in paint

When you're looking for a beautiful soft blue, look at pale grays that are on the blue side. If you're after a rich, chambray blue, choose a blue that isn't too green or too purple. If your heart is set on pink, but you fear a cloying cotton-candy effect, opt for a light pink with slight brownish undertones. For a not-too-minty green, choose one with a big dose of yellow; to avoid a green that is too sage, explore shades that don't have too much black in the mix, making it appear dingy gray. For a lovely mellow yellow, remember to avoid hues that are too buttery (too much orange) or too citrusy (too much green); you'll find the perfect yellow somewhere in the middle.

get the look: PREPPY ECLECTIC

Touches of modern mix with vintage, preppy, and downright cool to define this offbeat, yet dynamic, nursery. Consistent touches of orange anchor the mix and unify disparate styles and touches. A confident and unique hand is evident in this inventive nursery.

focal point >> BEDDING

The bold plaid and pops of orange in the crib bedding set the tone for this hip, preppy space.

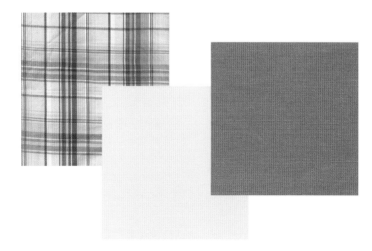

Painted ceiling: The paint treatment in this room is a fresh solution. Consider high wainscoting painted white, with a dash of color overhead, or basic white walls, crown molding, and a colored ceiling.

Tip: CEILINGS PAINTED SHADES OF BLUE ARE ESPECIALLY EFFECTIVE, AS THEY IMPLY "AIRINESS" AND GIVE A NOD TO THE SKIES.

Overhead light: This modern light fixture is an unexpected and fabulous touch that keeps this room from becoming predictable.

Crib & bed: The crib bedding was customized to match that of the full bed, already present in this space. Placing a bed in the nursery can prove very handy for mom.

chapter six
art & accessories

ARTWORK | MIRRORS & MOBILES | DECORATIVE ACCESSORIES
LIGHTING | GET THE LOOK

YOU'VE CHOSEN YOUR KEY FURNISHINGS AND SETTLED ON YOUR WALL TREATMENT. CONGRATULATIONS! You've done most of the hard work. Now it's time for pure fun. Selecting artwork and accessories for your baby's room should be an enjoyable and creative process. This is another opportunity to infuse the space with personality and make your nursery unique. Remember to stay true to what you love, to what inspires you and holds meaning for you. You'll spend oh-so-many early-morning hours staring at these four walls as you nurse and soothe your little one. Make sure you'll be gazing at something you adore.

The objects that you hang on your walls and from your ceiling and that you place throughout the room should communicate your vision for this one-of-a-kind nursery, rather than simply fill the space. With that in mind, consider transplanting your favorite pieces from other parts of the house. Maybe that charming flea-market still life of garden roses hanging in your hallway complements your chosen nursery wallpaper. Or perhaps that colorful piece of modern art from the living room picks up the blue in your walls and offsets the sweetness of the handcrafted Mexican bluebird mobile you've hung above the crib. Try moving that gorgeous, gold-leafed sunburst mirror from the foyer to the nursery; it could look playful and chic in your baby's Modern Nursery, echoing your oval-shaped crib with the bold polka-dot bedding. That curvy, textured white ceramic

"The objects you hang on your walls and place throughout the room should communicate your vision for this one-of-a-kind nursery."

lamp from the living room could help set the right sophisticated tone atop your child's sleek white lacquered Art Deco dresser. Or perhaps you want to treasure hunt for nursery artwork. The Internet is a great place to begin your search, as are antique stores and flea markets. Of course, baby and children's stores offer a wide selection of "nursery-appropriate" pieces, but keep in mind that they are also the traditional choice for many parents—one reason so many nurseries look alike. We suggest thinking outside of the nursery box and finding unusual pieces that resonate with you.

EMBROIDERED PAJAMAS WITH AN ASIAN MOTIF AREN'T JUST FOR LOUNGING: SHOW OFF YOUR FINDS AS IF THEY WERE HANGING IN A FAVORITE BABY SHOP.

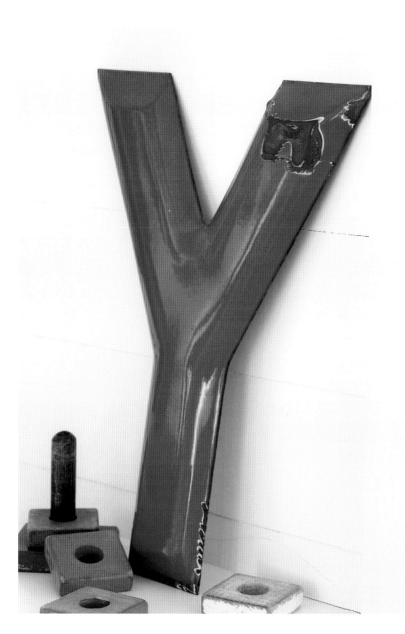

ONE MAN'S JUNK? THESE FLEA-MARKET FINDS CLEARLY BECOME TREASURES WHEN ACCESSORIZING THIS BOY'S VINTAGE NURSERY.

THE VINTAGE FLORAL OIL PAINTING ECHOES THE ROSE-PRINT WALLPAPER.

artwork

By searching the many online galleries or wandering your favorite haunts, you can find existing paintings, framed posters, collages, and the like that speak to your sensibility. Artwork for a child's room doesn't have to feature cutesy renditions of little lambs or cartoon characters. A beautifully realized portrait of the family dogs, for example, sets a stylish tone in the nursery.

Keep in mind that you can also commission pieces. A decorative artist can pull a graphic motif from your bedding, perhaps by "exploding" a floral pattern into a larger version for the walls. Or the artist could

"Artwork for a child's room doesn't have to feature cutesy renditions of little lambs or cartoon characters."

create an image that supports your focal point and render it as a striking pair of hanging panels or as a mural. If, for example, your chosen focal point is a collection of vintage Eiffel Tower statuettes, a decorative artist could create wall panels depicting the lovely rows of lollipop trees from the Tuileries Gardens.

You can also create your own artwork out of meaningful family photographs and drawings. Unifying these seemingly disparate visual elements depends on the framing. A collection of portraits of your newborn will look cohesive when showcased in large mattes and identical frames. We have one friend who created her nursery focal point by professionally framing the baby photographs of close relatives in simple white box frames for her Classic Nursery. Frames can also introduce an element of the unexpected. For example, a child's

A COLORFUL MODERN CANVAS LIVENS UP ANY SPACE AND KEEPS ITS APPEAL AS YOUR CHILD GROWS.

painting accented by a baroque gilded frame can feel totally fresh, offbeat, and personal.

Beautifully crafted baby items, such as an intricately embroidered dress, crocheted booties, or a handmade doll, can also serve as decoration for the nursery. Keepsakes that have been passed down through the family can be placed in shadow-box frames to be preserved and displayed. The sumptuous materials, elaborate detailing, and workmanship of such pieces often make them the perfect finishing touches to a nursery.

design tip:

If your design budget doesn't have room for framing art, improvise. Try fastening metal clipboard-style hooks to the corners of a print and then mounting it on nails; or use old-fashioned wooden clothes hooks to hang small prints from a clothesline suspended on a wall.

NO. 7

A COLLECTION OF FAMILY BABY PORTRAITS IS PARADED ALONG THE WALL ABOVE THE PANELING OF A BLUE-AND-WHITE ROOM.

above: TO CREATE CONTRAST WITH COLORED WALLS, **HANG FRAMED BLACK-AND-WHITE ART,** SUCH AS THESE ANIMAL AND BUG PRINTS.

right: **A PORTRAIT OF MAN'S BEST FRIEND** ALLOWS YOUR LITTLE ONE TO GET TO KNOW THE FAMILY PET.

Put your child's stamp on the
walls with silhouettes. Photograph
baby's profile, trace it on paper,
cut it out, and then paint around
the template. Another option:
Send the photo to one of several
online companies that will print
a silhouette on paper and
then return it to you for framing.

NO. 8

art ideas

- Does your older child, niece, or nephew have a knack? Consider commissioning one or all of them to make a series of works of art for your nursery.

- Use shadow boxes to frame three-dimensional artwork, such as paper flowers, vintage matchbox cars, or your old baby shoes.

- Create your own mobile with photographs or cut paper shapes. Blank mobiles with clips make this project easy and changeable.

- Shop flea markets for one-of-a-kind art, keeping an open mind and an understanding of the importance of a good reframing job.

- Make your own art. Whether it's rough or refined, art by the parents is the most special kind.

- Hang a beautiful vintage textile, such as your grandmother's quilt, a silk sari from India, or a colorful patterned scarf. For smaller, more delicate items, consider a lovely frame to protect and preserve.

- Group family photographs in unified frames. Pictures of aunts, cousins, you as a baby, grandparents, and other important people tell the story of where baby comes from and hold meaning for you as well.

- Alphabet cards and flash cards have been around for generations. An online-auction search can turn up countless interesting options for an educational and unique grouping or border around the room.

top right: **DISPLAY ARTWORK CREATED BY BABY'S SIBLINGS.**

bottom right: **TRY YOUR OWN ARTISTIC HAND ON CANVAS**—NOTHING IS MORE MEANINGFUL THAN CREATING YOUR OWN ART.

mirrors & mobiles

From the time they are born, babies begin a nonstop visual exploration of the world. For that reason, mirrors and mobiles find an appreciative home in the nursery. Mirrors splash light into the baby's room, and little ones delight in peering at themselves in looking glasses. Mirrors can also support your design message. Beveled and timeworn mirrors feel vintage; geometric shapes and clean lines feel modern. Mirrors framed by such textured, exotic materials as bamboo and rattan add an international feel. To lend an air of wit and breeziness to an Eclectic Nursery, a baroque carved mirror could be transformed with a coat of paint, either white or a pop of color, to contrast with your furnishings.

Mobiles hung above the crib engage and calm a baby. Keep in mind that with the myriad choices now on the market, you don't have to settle for a cutesy mobile if your chosen design message is chic. One quick search on the Internet will turn up dozens of fresh and artfully designed mobiles for baby's room. Take your time to select one that communicates your design message and pleases you as much as it will amuse your child. You can also create a mobile of your own choosing by using a kit (available on many Web sites or in baby boutiques); be sure to choose items of similar weight so the mobile balances. Alternatively, you can hang decorative elements, such as paper lanterns, individually from the ceiling above the crib.

BLACK-AND-WHITE CLOSE-UPS OF FAMILY MEMBERS ARE PASTED TO A VANITY MIRROR. A WOODEN FISH MOBILE IS REFLECTED IN THE GLASS.

PRETTY LANTERNS IN BOLD COLORS MAKE FOR A DELIGHTFUL VIEW FROM THE CRIB.

GOLDEN MIRRORS BRING REGAL RADIANCE INTO A SPACE.

"*Mirrors splash light
into the baby's room.*"

Art & Accessories Safety:

*While artwork makes a beautiful accent near the crib, make
sure that it is securely fastened to the wall so that it cannot be pulled
down by tiny grasping hands; better yet, keep all heavy items,
such as lamps, bookshelves, and paintings, well away from the crib.*

decorative accessories

Well-chosen decorative accessories can be the icing on the cake that is your beautiful nursery. Accessories can pull together and punctuate the look you are trying to achieve. It's easy to fall in love with many items, harder to pare down your choices to a bare minimum. But remember, clutter is not what you're after, especially when you consider how much more your baby is going to accumulate.

During these precious months of pregnancy, you'll no doubt receive a dazzling number of gifts for the nursery. Our suggestion to you: Edit, edit, edit! Indeed, be as ruthless as Attila the Hun might be if he were decorating a room. Purchase and keep only the pieces that work with your vision, or those items that have particular meaning to you. Exchange some for items that you love and donate the rest to a worthy charity. Forget about trying to please every well-meaning gift-giver and remember that you are the one who will be spending the most time in the nursery.

When displaying decorative items, look for one common thread, whether it be color, shape, or theme, to link all the pieces. Color unifies disparate elements into a collection. A group of naive animal-shaped ceramics,

"Color unifies disparate elements into a collection."

for example, makes a statement when all are white or celadon green. Also, try to vary shape and scale to create visual interest. The pieces should be pleasing to the eye and create a harmonious tableau, rather than feel like grouped clutter or bric-a-brac. Arranging your collection on a tasteful tray will further unify the items. If your vignette makes you happy, then it's successful!

Decorative Accessories Safety:

Make sure all items are out of reach unless they are intended for playing. Many items not intended and designed for babies can pose choking hazards.

THESE WHIPSTITCHED MINI-MOCCASINS WITH A SURPRISE INSIDE ARE FETCHING PROPS FOR ACCESSORIZING A DRESSER TOP OR ARMOIRE.

design tip:

Put on your designer's hat and go
hunting for decorative props.
How do you get inspired? Pretend
the room is going to be
photographed by your favorite
home-design magazine.

NO.9

left: **TOYS DO DOUBLE DUTY AS PROPS AND NECESSITIES.**

above: **START A DOLL COLLECTION,** STAGING YOUR SHELVES WITH
COLORFUL BABUSHKAS AND OTHER LADIES OF THE WORLD.

lighting

"That yellow-ducky lamp, while cute, is not your only option."

Using chandeliers, sconces, and lamps is a great way to accessorize the nursery with functional items. Chandeliers can accentuate your design message and lend great presence to your room, while also providing a light source for storybook reading. Wall sconces run the gamut of styles and eliminate the need for support furniture that might clutter the room. Table and floor lamps made especially for children's rooms can lend a whimsical touch, but allow yourself to experiment with lighting choices pulled from the rest of the house. That yellow-ducky lamp, while cute, is not your only option. You'll be surprised at how perfect that shatterproof crystal lamp looks on the bookcase, next to baby's favorite stuffed animals.

Keep in mind that a warm glow from several light sources creates a cozier effect than does lighting from one fixture. Abundant adjustable lighting is preferable to a too-dim room. Install a dimmer switch for your main lighting source so you can adjust its brightness, as you will no doubt be called to the nursery during the early-morning and late-night hours. A lamp next to your glider is a must; another essential is a lighting source, either wall sconces or a lamp, near the crib.

Lighting Safety:

Keep cords tucked out of sight, and, for an added dose of neatness and flair, tie up too-long cords with color-coordinated ribbon. In recent years, ophthalmologists have recommended against nightlights in children's rooms (the artificially extended daylight can cause abnormal development in the eyes).

right: **CRYSTAL CHANDELIERS** OFTEN LIVE IN A ROOM BEFORE BABY ARRIVES AND CAN BE A GLAMOROUS FOCAL POINT WHEN CENTERED IN THE SPACE. (NOTE: CHANDELIERS SHOULD NEVER BE HUNG DIRECTLY ABOVE A CRIB.)

far right (top): **SCANDINAVIANS ARE SAVVY** WITH LIGHTING SOLUTIONS, INCLUDING THIS MOUNTED FLOWER DESIGN CONSISTING OF FOLDED PLASTIC PETALS.

far right (bottom): **A METAL PINUP SCONCE** PROVIDES EXCELLENT OVERHEAD READING LIGHT FOR BEDTIME STORIES.

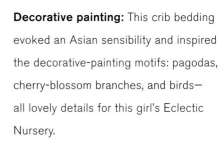

get the look: BOHEMIAN

Note the exotic touches and bohemian flair of this room. Motifs from the crib bedding—a delicate bird and cherry-tree branch—extend onto the wall in the form of a graceful mural. This nursery's Eastern panache calls for uncommon accessories from around the globe. Layers of pattern jazz up the room with eclectic texture.

focal point » PAINTED CRIB

We painted the crib salmon pink, a provocative spark against celadon-green walls. This shock of color makes the room feel distinctive and surprising and ties the crib to the coloring of the bedding and decorative accessories.

Tip: CAN'T FIND THE CRIB YOU WANT IN YOUR PERFECT SHADE? PAINT IT YOURSELF OR HIRE A PROFESSIONAL. ANY SEMIGLOSS WALL PAINT CAN TURN A CLASSIC CRIB INTO AN AUDACIOUS STATEMENT.

Decorative painting: This crib bedding evoked an Asian sensibility and inspired the decorative-painting motifs: pagodas, cherry-blossom branches, and birds—all lovely details for this girl's Eclectic Nursery.

Armoire: Why buy an armoire from a children's store when you have a world of design choices available? Here, a Chinese wedding cabinet (readily available in the marketplace) stores baby essentials in style.

Rugs: For bohemian flair, try layering pattern on pattern and smaller rug over larger rug.

conclusion: your nursery & the future

As you rock in your glider with your newborn in your arms, enjoying the beautiful nursery you've created, you will probably not believe what we're about to say: Sometime all too soon, your baby will grow into a toddler, and then a child, with opinions and preferences all his or her own. Your child's bedroom will then need to evolve, too.

Of course, decorating can be costly and time-consuming, so choose your nursery's base decor and furnishings with longevity in mind. Buy the most durable, highest-quality items you can afford, and select pieces sophisticated enough to suit a growing child's taste. Well-made curtains and rugs cut from ageless fabrics and materials will enjoy a greater lifespan. You might also opt for furnishings that have been created to accommodate a child's growth from baby to toddler. There are many tastefully designed cribs that convert into toddler beds with the addition of conversion kits. What's more, some of these beds take into consideration a maturing child's need for self-expression and choice. A number of conversion kits offer a variety of finials (decorative knobs for the bedposts), which allows a little one to select an airplane, star, or flower motif, depending on his or her budding sensibilities. Finding suitable bedding to adapt to the room as your child develops should not prove difficult, either. Choose toddler and twin bedding that comes

design tip:

If you have the space, keep a
twin- or full-size bed in the
baby's room for nursing, cuddling,
reading, and changing. Then
it will be ready for your baby as
he outgrows his crib and
toddler bed.

NO. 10

"Buy the most durable, highest-quality items you can afford."

in colors and styles compatible to your crib set, so you can deftly match your room's color palette, even as your child grows.

Many changing tables on the market come with a removable lip, necessary to keep a changing pad firmly in place. By simply pulling the lip off, the changer seamlessly becomes a big-kid dresser. When searching for a nursery armoire, keep in mind that this piece should have decades of life ahead of it. Choose stylish, timeless details and high-quality construction. A professional paint job and a simple changing of knobs or pulls can take a handsome piece into the teenage years, with secret diaries and high-school sweatshirts taking the place of the baby blankets and diapers.

With the near-future in mind, you can purchase a double-glider or a family rocker instead of a single-glider. Such a chair will not only suit a mother and her nursing infant, it will also accommodate a parent and a growing toddler for nightly story-time. At that point, you will want to place a well-stocked bookshelf within arm's reach and add a stylish floor lamp, too. To keep your child's room clutter-free, consider packing up outgrown clothing every three months and toys no longer age appropriate every six months. You might have a friend or relative whose younger child would be a happy recipient of such items, or you could store such items away in airtight plastic boxes in anticipation of your next child.

A PRETTY PAINTING AND FRENCH-STYLE FURNITURE ARE ELEMENTS WITH STAYING POWER IN AN EVOLVING NURSERY.

Artwork selection easily evolves with a young one's taste. You can swiftly exchange baby-specific paintings and photographs for decorative touches that reflect your child's preferences; you could also hang his own artwork. Guide your child gently and wisely as he stretches his aesthetic wings, allowing your little one to make a few mistakes on the path to self-expression. You've planted the seeds of good taste with your lovely nursery. And ultimately, like mother's milk, a sound design sense flows from parent to child. Our one last piece of advice: Children are a precious gift. Remember to enjoy every moment with your baby in comfort and in beauty.

CHANGING TABLES WITH DRAWERS STORE TOYS AND BLANKETS NOW, AND PERHAPS SOCCER UNIFORMS LATER.

A PAINTED ARMOIRE HOUSES DRESSES, PILLOWS, TOYS, AND SHOES, AND ADAPTS EASILY TO CHANGES.

resources

JONATHAN ADLER

2133 Fillmore Street
San Francisco, CA 94115
(415) 563-9500
www.jonathanadler.com
Home furnishings

CRISPINA

40 Melville Street
Pittsfield, MA 01201
(413) 637-0075
www.crispina.com
Handcrafted textiles

GIGGLE

2110 Chestnut Street
San Francisco, CA 94123
(415) 440-9034
www.egiggle.com
Baby furnishings

NANCY KOLTES

800 Redwood Highway, Suite 211
Mill Valley, CA 94941
(415) 924-5811
www.nancykoltes.com
Linens and furnishings

LAVISH

540 Hayes Street
San Francisco, CA 94102
(415) 565-0540
www.shoplavish.com
Home accessories

THE LITTLE FISH BOUTIQUE

320 West Portal Avenue
San Francisco, CA 94127
(415) 681-7242
Home accessories

LOTUS BLEU

327 Hayes Street
San Francisco, CA 94102
(415) 861-2700
www.lotusbleudesign.com
*Art and interior design;
home accessories*

MAISON D'ETRE

5640 College Avenue
Oakland, CA 94618
(510) 658-2901
www.maisondetre.com
Home accessories

**MILL VALLEY BABY
& KIDS CO.**

12 Miller Avenue
Mill Valley, CA 94941
(415) 389-1312
www.mvbabyandkids.com
Baby and children's furnishings

MUDPIE

1694 Union Street
San Francisco, CA 94123
(415) 771-9262
Children's clothing and furnishings

NEST

2300 Fillmore Street
San Francisco, CA 94115
(415) 292-6199
Home furnishings and accessories

**PAST PERFECT DESIGN
COLLECTIVE**

2230 Union Street
San Francisco, CA 94123
(415) 929-7651
Antique and vintage furnishings

SUMMER HOUSE

21 Throckmorton Avenue
Mill Valley, CA 94941
(415) 383-6695
Clothing, furnishings, and accoutrements

TAMALPAIS GENERAL STORE

23 Throckmorton Avenue
Mill Valley, CA 94941
(415) 388-7437
Everything under the sun

ERICA TANOV

2408 Fillmore Street
San Francisco, CA 94115
(415) 674-1228
www.ericatanov.com
Clothing and home accessories

TIMELESS TREASURES

2176 Sutter Street
San Francisco, CA 94115
(415) 775-8366
www.timelesstreasuressf.com
Vintage furnishings and findings

ZEBRA HALL

(800) 834-9165
www.zebrahall.com
Toys and games

ZINC DETAILS

1905 Fillmore Street
2410 California Street
San Francisco, CA 94115
(415) 776-9003
www.zincdetails.com
Modern furnishings

services

**LUANNE BRADLEY
DESIGN STUDIO**

201 San Fernando Way
San Francisco, CA 94127
(415) 640-8684
Staging, prop rental, and interior design

**FAY WYLES—DECORATIVE
PAINTING**

(415) 299-0838
www.designsbyfay.com
*Decorative painting and artwork
by commission*

Acknowledgments

To our tireless photo-shoot team: Wendi Nordeck, Alana Springs, Luanne Bradley, Nick Allen, Deborah Sherman, Shannon Flood, Mary Crofton, Mike Dugan, Max Lopez, Fay Wyles, and Sharon Corbett. You made this book come to life, and are truly the heroes.

To our homeowners, who opened up their beautiful homes to support this project: May these photographs be treasured for years to come, and may the memory of your houses overtaken be long forgotten. The Barish family—San Francisco, CA; the Berger family—Santa Rosa, CA; the Bradley family—San Francisco, CA; the Sarosi family—Mill Valley, CA; the Lehman family—San Francisco, CA; the Patell family—San Francisco, CA; the Tobin family—Tiburon, CA. Your graciousness and generosity was immeasurable. Thank you.

To Lisa Campbell, Jennifer Sparkman, Doug Ogan, Evan Hulka, Tera Killip, and Brooke Johnson at Chronicle Books, who have patiently and skillfully guided us through this watershed project.

To Alison Gee, our writer, who interpreted our ramblings seamlessly—as if by magic. You are truly an artist.

To Luanne Bradley, project manager and all-around maven: You truly made it all come together. You're incredible.

To Sharon Corbett and Chris Sutter, whose skills, dedication, and all-around good nature enable our spontaneity and bring our ideas to life.

To the book's graphic designer, Satoko Furuta, whose brilliant design vision on the page has proven to be an essential extension of our own vision.

To the stores in San Francisco and Marin (see Resources) that partnered with us to put the "Style" in "Nursery Style."

To our employees at Serena & Lily, who kept the ship afloat while this book was being made: We could not have done it without you.

To Lily's children—Max, Zeke, and Nate, who have allowed their rooms to be torn apart and naps disturbed by one-too-many photo shoots.

And to the one and only Alana Springs: Thank you for your devotion, your humility, your tirelessness, and your vision. You're a member of the family, in all regards.

index

A

Accessories, 115–16, 129–31
Architectural features, 41
Armoires
  alternatives for, 134
  as changing table, 59
  choosing, 138
  for storage, 71, 75, 139
Art
  alternatives to framing, 119
  commissioning, 118
  creating, 118–19, 123
  ideas for, 118–23
  safety and, 127
  selecting, 115–16, 118, 139

B

Baby photographs, 118, 119
Baskets, 71
Bedding
  choosing, 85–86, 136, 138
  as focal point, 34, 85, 112
  safety and, 86
  texture of, 81
Beds, 112, 137. *See also* Cribs; Daybeds
Blankets, 82, 85–86
Bookshelves, 63, 71
Boy's room
  bedding for, 83
  color palette for, 44
Bumpers, 85, 86

C

Carpeting, 93, 96
Ceiling, painted, 103, 112
Chairs, 64, 67–68, 136

Changing tables
  alternatives for, 59, 60, 63
  checklist for, 61
  choosing, 59
  converting, into dresser, 138
  with drawers, 139
  safety and, 63
  size of, 59
Classic Nursery
  characteristics of, 18
  color palette for, 44, 45
  crib for, 56
  examples of, 18, 41, 78
  mood and, 30
Clothing, storage for, 71
Colorists, 110
Color palette
  choosing, 44–45, 109–11
  classic, 18
  eclectic, 25
  as focal point, 42–43, 98
  gender and, 44–45
  modern, 23
  mood and, 42–43
  vintage, 20
Cribs
  choosing, 52
  convertible, 52, 136
  drop gate vs. fixed rail, 52, 54
  as focal point, 134
  painting, 134
  safety and, 54
  same color as wall, 78
  shape of, 52
  styles of, 52, 56–57
Crib skirts, 85
Curtains, 88, 91

D

Daybeds, 64, 67
Design
  allowing time for, 13
  direction, 15
  focal point, 33–34, 36, 39, 41–43, 46, 48
  researching, 29
  strategy for, 47
Desks, 63
Diaper receptacle, 61
Dressers
  as changing table, 59, 63
  converting changing table into, 138
  pulls for, 72
  for storage, 71

E

Eclectic Nursery
  characteristics of, 25
  color palette for, 44, 45
  crib for, 57
  examples of, 25, 34, 39, 112, 134

F

Flokati, 95
Flooring, 93–96
Focal points
  architecture as, 41
  bedding as, 34, 85, 112
  choosing, 46
  color palette as, 42–43, 98
  crib as, 134
  decorative painting as, 78
  definition of, 33
  heirloom as, 39
  walls as, 26, 36
Furniture. *See also individual pieces*
  amount of, 51
  longevity and, 136

main actions for, 51

repurposing vintage, 43

safety and, 68

G

Gender

color palette and, 44–45

impact of, 30

Girl's room, color palette for, 45

Gliders, 64, 67, 81, 138

H

Heirlooms, 39

K

Keepsakes, 119

L

Lighting, 132

M

Mirrors, 124, 126, 127

Mobiles, 123, 124, 126

Modern Nursery

characteristics of, 23

color palette for, 44, 45

crib for, 57

examples of, 23, 36

mood and, 29–30

Molding, 101, 104

Mood

color palette and, 42–43

style vs., 29–30

N

Nightlights, 132

Nightstands, 72

O

Ottomans, 64, 136

P

Paint

choosing color of, 109–11

lead-based, 68

sampling, 111

Painting, decorative

advantages of, 101, 104, 106

choosing motif for, 134

as focal point, 78

Paneling, 101, 103, 105

Patterns, 104, 106–7

Photographs, 118, 119, 123, 126

Polka dots, 38, 107

Q

Quilts, 82, 85, 86

R

Research, 29

Rocking chairs, 64

Roman shades, 88

Rugs

advantages of, 93

cleaning, 95

as focal point, 48

layering, 134

safety and, 96

styles of, 95

texture of, 81

S

Safety

accessories and, 129

art and, 127

bedding and, 86

changing tables and, 63

cribs and, 54

furniture and, 68

lighting and, 132

rugs and, 96

window treatments and, 91

Shadow boxes, 123

Sheets. *See* Bedding

Shutters, 88

Silhouettes, 78, 122

Storage, 71–77

Style. *See also* Classic Nursery;

Eclectic Nursery; Modern Nursery;

Vintage Nursery

classifications of, 15

defining your, 13, 15

T

Tablecloths, 83

Toys, storage for, 71, 76, 77

V

Vintage Nursery

characteristics of, 20

color palette for, 45

crib for, 56

examples of, 20, 26, 48, 98

W

Wallpaper

advantages of, 106

effect of, 101, 104

as focal point, 26, 36

Walls

as focal point, 26, 36

impact of, 101

matching, to textiles, 103–4

painted, 108–11

patterns on, 104, 106–7

polka dots on, 38, 107

white, 103

Window treatments

options for, 88, 90

safety and, 91

texture of, 81